VIOLIN
LESSONS

ARNOLD ZABLE

TEXT PUBLISHING MELBOURNE AUSTRALIA

The Text Publishing Company acknowledges the Traditional Owners of the country on which we work, the Wurundjeri people of the Kulin Nation, and pays respect to their Elders past and present.

textpublishing.com.au

The Text Publishing Company
Wurundjeri Country, Level 6, Royal Bank Chambers, 287 Collins Street,
Melbourne Victoria 3000 Australia

First published by The Text Publishing Company, 2011
This edition published 2012
Reprinted 2023

Cover art and design by WH Chong
Page design by Susan Miller
Typeset by J&M Typesetters
Printed and bound in Australia by Griffin Press, an Accredited ISO AS/NZS 14001:2004 Environmental Management System printers

National Library of Australia
Cataloguing-in-Publication entry

Author: Zable, Arnold.

Title: Violin lessons / Arnold Zable.

ISBN: 9781921922787 (pbk.)
ISBN: 9781921961588 (ebook.)

Subjects: Zable, Arnold--Travel.
          Voyages and travels.
          Families.

Dewey Number: 304.8

This project has been assisted by the Commonwealth Government through the Australia Council, its arts and advisory body.

The paper this book is printed on is certified against the Forest Stewardship Council' Standards. Griffin Press holds chain of custody certification SCS-COC-001185. FSC' promotes environmentally responsible, socially beneficial and economically viable management of the world's forests.

Arnold Zable is a highly acclaimed novelist, storyteller and educator. His books include *Jewels and Ashes*, *The Fig Tree*, *Café Scheherazade*, *Scraps of Heaven* and *Sea of Many Returns*. Arnold is a human rights advocate and president of the International PEN, Melbourne. He lives in Melbourne with his wife and son.

arnoldzable.com

Dedicated to Amal Basry, and the 353

He holds him with his glittering eye—
The Wedding-Guest stood still,
And listens like a three years' child:
The Mariner hath his will.

The Rime of the Ancient Mariner
SAMUEL TAYLOR COLERIDGE

CONTENTS

Violin Lessons

I received a violin on a recent birthday. It had been forty years since I last played and my first attempts to resume were not promising. I could not produce a sound. I had forgotten that a bow requires rosin to adhere to the strings. When I placed the instrument on my left shoulder, the collarbone bore the stress. My fingers, wrists and forearms ached. Muscles long dormant were rudely awakened.

Slowly the basic skills returned. My bow movements became more controlled. Like homing pigeons, my fingers found their way back to the correct positions. Scales and arpeggios I had once diligently practised became fluent again. The music notations regained their meaning and evoked the memory of sheets propped against the wall on a kitchen sideboard.

The sink beside the sideboard was stained with rusted enamel, the linoleum warped and cracked. Hadassah, my mother and faithful audience of one, sat by the table preparing the evening meal. She nodded her head in approval, which was no guide to the quality of the playing. The fact that a son of hers was learning the violin was enough cause for pleasure. She spoke often, and with reverence, of the night she had attended a recital by the teenage prodigy Yehudi Menuhin on world tour. She was a woman who watched every penny, yet willingly drew on limited funds to pay for my lessons. But she did not know that my teacher, Mr Offman, was a tyrant.

Mr Offman taught violin and piano from his house on the corner of Rathdowne and Pigdon streets. I set out once a week, violin in hand, on the twenty-minute walk to the house, and strolled home after the lesson, relieved the ordeal was over. I felt more at home in the streets than inside Mr Offman's music room.

After three years of lessons I took part in a concert. I played 'Long, Long Ago' and 'Ave Maria'. Judging by the applause, the audience was pleased with my efforts. I bowed awkwardly and left the stage thankful I had performed without obvious error.

After the concert, Mr Offman congratulated me in the foyer. He had never before praised my efforts. He had, it seemed, forgotten the many times he struck me over the back of the neck with his bow in response to my musical transgressions. Three years, I thought, three arduous years it had taken to produce a word of praise. I contemplated the humourless years ahead and, in my moment of triumph, decided to give up playing.

Years later, I portrayed Mr Offman in one of my novels as

Mr Spielvogel, a musician who had performed in pre-war Austria, a post-war immigrant embittered by his loss of status, a teacher who longed for the music salons of Vienna.

I drew on my memories to recreate his corner house as a ghostly replica of past glories. I lined the passage with photos of musicians dressed in tuxedos and bow ties, instruments poised by their sides. I placed portraits of Arnold Schoenberg and Gustav Mahler on the music room walls, and assumed that Spielvogel's vocation as a musician had been thwarted by the Nazi occupation and the horrors it had visited upon his people. I did not know then that Mr Offman's journey was far more exotic than the one I had imagined.

Not long after the novel was published I was invited to discuss it at a Sunday morning book club. When the formal discussion was over one of those present introduced himself as Naji Cohen. He had taken up the violin many years ago and performed in a Baghdad orchestra. He still possessed his original instrument. Would I like to see it, and would I like to hear the story of its journey?

Weeks later I approached the townhouse to which he and his wife Myra had retired. Naji did not waste time on pleasantries. He had a tale and he was eager to tell it. He tilted his head towards me as he talked, leaning forward, in a gesture of communion.

His lifelong obsession began one afternoon in 1940 when he was ten years old. He was walking home from school through the streets of a Baghdad suburb when he was stopped by the sound of a violin. The Arabic music emanated from the balcony of a two-storey house. Naji was captivated.

'Ya Allah, I swear to God, that first time I stopped and listened, it clicked with me,' he says. 'All my life belongs to that moment. Would you believe it? I stood there for an hour. I did not want to leave. I went crazy on it.'

For two years Naji followed the same route home from school and stopped by the house to listen. The player was a violin teacher known as Blind Jamil. Every afternoon, at the same time, it was his habit to play his violin on the balcony.

Naji pleaded with his father, a well-to-do merchant, to allow him to take lessons. His father refused. Don't be stupid, he argued. Music was a lowly job fit only for itinerants and drifters. It would take time away from his studies. He had plans for his son to study in America and had set his sights on him becoming an eye doctor. Baghdad was not for his son. Baghdad was the past, not the future.

'Ya Allah, a father had absolute power at that time,' says Naji. 'He told me to stop thinking about the violin, but whenever I passed by Blind Jamil's and heard him playing, I became crazy with it.'

Naji saved up and secretly bought a violin from the musician. The arguments resumed, and with greater force, until his father could no longer abide his entreaties. He allowed him to take lessons as long as they did not interfere with his studies.

Once a week Naji climbed the narrow spiral staircase to the upper room. 'I can see it now,' he says, eyes narrowing. 'I swear it.' He stretches out his arms, and extends his fingers as if touching the memory. Naji does not know the details of Jamil's life, whether he was married or single. He cannot remember the layout of his rooms. He recalls only the spiral staircase, his conduit to the lessons. 'Ya Allah, I was only interested in the music.'

Blind Jamil would greet him, feel his way to a chair and begin his instructions. He wore dark glasses and was dressed informally in an open-necked shirt and trousers. He taught him as he had been taught to play, by ear.

At fourteen, Naji was invited to join a circle of young musicians. They called themselves *Ansar el Musika*, the Lovers of Music. 'This is how I translate it,' says Naji. 'That is what Ansar means for me. We were crazy about Arabic music.'

There were ten players in the ensemble: five violinists, a cellist, a tabla player, a duff player, an oud player and a singer. The singer was a Muslim, the rest were Jewish. At first they played only for themselves. They met in each other's homes several nights a week. They ate and drank, and played until the early hours of the morning. 'That's all. Only music. We had no other subject to deal with.'

To expand their repertoire, the group spent hours watching films featuring renowned Egyptian musicians. They studied each film, session after session until they had memorised every note. They invented their own system of notation with instructions to go faster, slow down, and so on.

Sometime in 1945, Ansar el Musika came to the attention of a Baghdad broadcaster. The musicians were offered a weekly half-hour radio program and they gained a loyal following. As their reputation grew they were asked to perform at private gatherings and celebrations. They travelled to Mosul, three hundred and fifty kilometres north of Baghdad, hired by a sheikh to perform at his daughter's wedding. They were driven to the reception through the streets in horse-drawn carriages, playing. People lined the footpaths, waving. The group performed before the guests for three days and three nights and lost track of the hours.

An avid fan of their radio program offered them the use of a houseboat on the Tigris River. The group practised every evening and partied until well past midnight. People in riverside homes sat on their balconies and listened. Strollers on the banks of the river would stop to listen.

On warm Baghdad nights, the group crossed over to an island. 'The people on the island caught the fish from the Tigris, cut it along the back, and split it clean in half. Like this,' says Naji, demonstrating with vigorous gestures. 'They washed it. Cleaned it. Sprinkled it with pepper and spices.'

He lifts his hands. 'Look, this is how it was done. My hands are the fish and each finger is a pole. They placed one fish on each pole, twenty fish at one time facing a wood fire. This is how they grilled them. We ate and drank, and played till four in the morning.

'Ya Allah,' says Naji, his eyes alight with the memory, 'Baghdad was a beautiful city. Directly opposite our house stood a mosque. I can see it now. I swear it. The cry of the muezzin woke me every morning. His prayers reminded me of the music played by Blind Jamil.'

Despite the semblance of peace, all was not well. Naji does not wish to dwell on the politics, the contested versions of the street battles, and on what brought his family's many years in the city to an end. 'Music and politics should not mix,' he insists. 'I loved Baghdad. I loved the music and my fellow musicians, but times changed when Israel became part of the equation: in 1949, there were mass demonstrations against the newly formed state. It was time to leave, and I left.'

This is all he wishes to say. 'They have their story and we have ours. We were only interested in making music.' I try to push it further. Naji refuses. He is resolute. Emphatic. 'The subject is music. If we are discussing music, I don't want to discuss any other subject.'

Naji travelled by train from Baghdad south to the confluence of the Tigris and Euphrates. He engaged smugglers in the city of Basra for the onward journey. He had with him Razi, a thirteen-year-old boy who had been entrusted to Naji by his family. They hid by day and moved by night, on foot and by donkey, following the course of the Shatt al-Arab waterway. On the third night, a smuggler rowed them to the opposite shore, and deposited them on the Iranian side.

'It's still in my head,' says Naji. 'I swear it. When the smuggler rowed we had to be quiet. Not a murmur. We were very nervous. The smuggler rowed so slowly no one could hear him. It was three o'clock in the morning. In the middle of the river there was an iron ball, two metres in diameter. He told us, this is the border. When we pass it we will be in Iran.

'He dumped us in no-man's-land. It was dark and freezing.

At five o'clock it started to get light. I saw women dressed in black abayas. They were walking on the beach. They carried jugs of water on their heads. They surrounded us, maybe thirty women. They called the police, who told us they would hand us back to the Iraqis if we did not give them our money. Razi was crying. He was hysterical. I emptied my pockets. In this moment you think only of survival. If they took us back over the waterway, we thought the border police would kill us.'

In his haste, Naji had left his violin in Baghdad. Two years later his family joined him in Tel Aviv, where he had settled after leaving Iran within months of his clandestine arrival. While the refugees from Iraq tried to smuggle out some of the wealth they had been ordered to leave behind, his sister brought only the violin. Naji had rung her up before she left Baghdad. 'I want nothing else,' he told her. 'I am lost without it.'

At that time the members of Ansar el Musika were spread throughout the land, one in Tel Aviv, another in Haifa, a third in Jerusalem. One by one they found each other. In 1955, they re-assembled and established the same group, except for the singer, who remained in Baghdad. They would gather to play every Friday.

Yet in the new state they remained outsiders. The Mizrahi Jews, the Easterners, as they were called, were not warmly welcomed. Many lived in tent cities and struggled to find employment. The trauma of displacement was compounded by their status as fringe dwellers. Arabic music was not appreciated. It was the music of newcomers who had to conform to the demands of a new country, an alien culture. The Lovers of Music confined their playing to their weekly gatherings.

'People did not want to hear our music,' says Naji. 'We found a place near Ramat Gan called the Hill of Napoleon. The hill was far from everyone. We had it all to ourselves. We could do as we liked, and play as long as we wanted. Every Friday night our friends brought food, folding chairs and blankets. One man brought crates of watermelons. Others brought Iraqi delicacies. The number of people who attended grew. For fifteen years we gathered at the same place every Friday. Just eat. Just drink. Just play, till four in the morning. That's all.'

Naji travelled to Melbourne in 1964. He left his wife Myra and one-year-old son in Tel Aviv while he explored his options. 'Ya Allah, the reasons I left are not so complicated. I wanted to dare myself to build a new life. I wanted to know what it is to be in a new country. My eyes were set on the future.'

Myra and their son joined him several months later. Naji entrusted his violin to a friend in Tel Aviv. 'Why? It is simple. A violin needs to be played. If an instrument is not played, it dies. My friend said why don't you leave it with me? He used it in my absence and kept it alive. I thought maybe I will bring it over in a year, but I was always busy. Time passes. Soon it is ten years. Then twenty. Then, would you believe it? It was almost forty years.'

Naji pauses. 'There is another reason I didn't bring the violin with me,' he says. 'I could not just sit and play by myself. It's not easy when for twenty years you have played with one group. They were my closest friends. I loved to play with them. How could I replace them? And who played Iraqi music here at that time?' He lifts his hands, palms facing upwards, and shrugs. 'I would have been playing alone.'

In 2002 Naji regained possession of the violin. 'Why? It is not so complicated. I was retired and had time on my hands. I visited my friends in Ramat Gan. Ramat Gan is now a little Baghdad. I swear it. In the coffeehouses you can hear the music I heard when I first stopped at Blind Jamil's. When people talk, they are waving their hands, like this, like Iraqi people. There is a family that sells mastic ice cream. The mastic is like chewing gum. It can stretch for half a metre without breaking. The recipe is a secret handed over from father to son. No one else knows how to make this.

'My friends supplied me with cassettes and videos, and I took the violin back to Melbourne. I was shy to hold it again. It was very strange. My fingers did not move. Then it started coming. Now I must play. My wife goes twice a week to play bridge. First I play. Then I put on the DVDs and videos of Arabic musicians.

'I listen to Umm Khultum, the great Egyptian singer. All the Arabic people loved her. They still love her, forty years after she has gone. When she goes deep into a song, it takes you. Completely. When she sings I must sing with her. Shout with her! Take my violin and play with her. God help me! Go crazy with her.

'For forty years I did not listen. I was busy bringing up my children. Now I spend hours, upstairs, in my music room. I shut the door, turn down the lights, turn on the tape and lie on the sofa, and listen. You get inside the music, and the music gets inside you. You see? There is no politics in it. Only music. You are back with your friends, in Baghdad, in Ramat Gan, on Napoleon's Hill. You are everywhere, and you are nowhere. You listen to each instrument, the oud, the duff, the cello, the flute and, of course, the violin. The instruments follow the singer like faithful servants. Ya Allah. It drives you crazy. Once I start, I cannot stop listening.'

Naji leads me up a flight of stairs from the lounge to the upper floor. Unlike Blind Jamil's spiral staircase the steps are spacious and polished. The music room is simply furnished with a sofa, a fold-back chair and built-in shelves stacked with CDs and cassettes. The room resembles a large cockpit. The windows slant outwards and a long desk runs the length of the room beneath them. It holds a CD player, cassette player, a turntable and a reel-to-reel recorder. Naji lays out jars of cashews and shelled almonds and offers me a whisky. He sits back at the controls and reaches for the violin.

'Would you believe it? This is the instrument I bought from Blind Jamil more than sixty years ago. The man who restored it told me it is a copy of a Stradivarius. It is for sure over one hundred years old. You can tell that the neck has cracked from the pressure of the strings. My friend in Tel Aviv reinforced the neck with metal. Look, he did a great job. The neck is stronger. But with just a small crack a violin loses value. Each blemish affects the sound.

'To be honest I am thinking of buying a new violin. I saw one the other day, without the case and bow, in St Petersburg, an antique shop in a lane off Collins Street. It is a French violin. It has a beautiful sound, but this one I will always keep.

'I touch it and remember the day of my first lesson with Blind Jamil. He did not teach me the correct style of holding it. He was a poor man, and he had taught himself how to play. He held the violin between the thumb and forefinger against the webbing. Like this. You see? You can't control the strings. The closeness to the neck restricts the movement of the fingers. I don't know how he played so well with this method. Now I hold it with a gap. Like this. I have more control. I changed to this style when I began playing with Ansar el Musika. They corrected me.'

He hands over the violin. His instrument brings out the desire to play. There is a lightness and resonance that I do not feel in my violin. I am embarrassed at my lack of artistry, and regret not having persisted with my lessons. I hand the violin back to Naji. He adjusts it on his shoulder. His fingers reach for the strings, and find their way to their places, tentatively at first, building up from uncertain beginnings. He closes his eyes. He is no longer present, but lost in the playing.

As he plays my thoughts turn back to Mr Offman. I recall the fluency I developed after months of practice, the dread with which I approached the lessons, and the relief I felt when I stepped out an hour later. I recall scenes I had long forgotten, of Mr Offman standing beside me, showing me how a violin should be played, instructing me and then playing. Offman, like Naji now, in full flight, forgetting himself, before coming to a sudden landing and opening his eyes to a room in a rented house, far from the scenes of his musical triumphs.

Naji is in a reverie. He bends over the violin and hums to the song he is playing. The music is hypnotic. It conveys me to long forgotten places. It awakens memories. I recall a recent remark of a friend I had not seen for decades. She had known Mr Offman and had read my account of him in the guise of Spielvogel. 'You have got him right in some ways,' she had said. 'But he did not live in pre-war Vienna. Instead he performed for many years in the Middle East.'

I began to make enquiries. All leads proved false until I did the obvious. I looked for the name in the phone book and found one Offman listed. A woman answered my call. 'My name is Rose,' she says. 'My husband, Sam, was Felix's son.' It was the first time I had heard my violin teacher called Felix. I had always known him as Mr Offman. 'My husband died two years ago,' Rose says. 'I know something of the family history, and I have photographs.'

The photos are on the kitchen table when I arrive the following morning. The oldest is a portrait of Felix as a young man, violin in hand, in the city of Lodz, circa 1930. The next image is of Felix and his wife Julia in Beirut, the Paris of the Middle East as its French occupiers called it. Julia is radiant. Felix's hair is black and slicked back. His face is unlined, his gaze direct and confident. He is dressed in a stylish suit, a dapper man at ease with the world.

There is a photo taken in Tehran of Felix playing clarinet as a member of a jazz quintet, and a photo of a band clustered around a female lead singer, a dog sprawled on the carpet before them. There is a shot captioned 'Tehran 1937': Felix is bending over towards Julia, who is holding their newborn son on a hospital bed. The couple appear secure and relaxed, firmly bonded.

Next is a photo of Felix squatting on the pavement in a

Beirut street beside his three children. Felix's young son, Sam, stands between Sonia and Mimi, identical twins with identical white bows in their hair. The girls are infants; the photo was taken in 1947.

The final image is of the Mr Offman I knew. His hair is greying, receding to the point of balding. He looks ill at ease, his confidence eroded. The photo evokes memories of my dread as I approached the Rathdowne Street house for my lessons.

Rose does not recall her father-in-law ever holding an instrument, neither clarinet nor violin. She never saw him seated at the piano, never heard him talk about music. Instead she has an enduring memory of him clutching a transistor to his ear, listening to the Saturday races, and bent over racing form guides, circling the names of horses. Her knowledge of his life is composed of fragments from conversations with her mother-in-law, Julia, who lived far longer than her husband.

Felix Offman was born in the Polish city of Czestochowa, Julia in Lodz. Felix played violin, clarinet and piano; Julia, classical piano. Rose knows little of their early life at that time. In the 1930s they left for the Middle East. Rose believes that during the war Felix was interned for two years in the Syrian city of Aleppo. She knows no other details. Apart from this interlude they led a life as musicians with stays in Beirut, Tehran and other Middle Eastern cities.

Sam and his father were both strong-willed men. They often argued. A child prodigy on piano, Sam had given up his music career at an early age, despite his love of performing. He never spoke of his father with emotion. He rarely spoke of him at all.

Yes, Felix was an ill-tempered man, Rose affirms, a hard task-master, but she admired his straight-talking ways.

Felix died in 1974. His daughters were overseas at the time. Sam helped carry the body out of the house with a member of the Chevra Kadisha, the Jewish burial society. Together they lifted him from the bed and placed him on a stretcher. Sam remained haunted for years by that final sight of his father, a frail man in pyjamas, stripped of his dignity in death as he had been stripped of his ambitions in life.

Rose provides the phone number of Mr Offman's daughter Mimi. The next afternoon I am again looking at black-and-white photos. Mimi regrets there are so few. I have not seen her since I stopped playing the violin. I recognise her and remember my first visit to the Rathdowne Street house, with my father, to be introduced to the music teacher.

Mr Offman was on his best behaviour for the occasion. I had not yet signed up. He called in the twins to demonstrate their skills. Sonia and Mimi entered politely, sat side by side at the piano and obliged with a duet. I was impressed by their fluency, but I sensed an air of uneasiness in the room, the awkward silence that greeted them, and the silence when they stood up from the piano before quickly leaving. My memory of the incident is vivid. Mimi does not recall it.

I lay out the photos like cards arranged for a hand of patience. Felix Offman stands at a microphone with two musicians in a Beirut cabaret on the Avenue des Francais; all three are clowning about. Felix plays the clarinet in a sextet in a nightclub. The band members are dressed in black bow ties and white tuxedoes. There are duplicates of photos Rose had shown me the previous day, and snaps of Julia and Felix in post-war Melbourne.

I am astonished to hear that when her father was alive, Mimi didn't know he had been a jazz musician. She had never known him to play in a band, or to play with anyone except his students. She knew him only as a classical violinist and pianist. She learned of his pre-war jazz career after his death. Just recently she too has become interested in jazz. She confirms that her father was an ill-tempered teacher who would rap her over the knuckles if her performance displeased him. After a time, she and her twin sister refused to be taught by him.

Like Rose, Mimi knows only fragments of her parents' pre-war life. Her mother once mentioned she had played piano for the silent movies in Lodz. She recalls nothing of her infancy in the Middle East, and has vague memories of their arrival in Melbourne in the final weeks of 1949.

In common with many immigrants of the time, they were taken straight from the ship by train hundreds of kilometres inland to the migrant camp of Bonegilla. The men and women were separated and directed to army barracks. Her father was assigned to a gang of road workers. He had asked to be allowed to wear gloves to protect his musician's hands. He had beautiful hands, says Mimi. The workers laughed at him.

After a year's stay, the family moved from Bonegilla to the city, and lived for a time in a rented room in Brunswick. Felix worked as a machinist in a hosiery factory and ran a clothing stall in the Victoria market. He taught piano and violin after the family shifted into the house on Rathdowne Street, but the fees for the lessons did not provide enough income. Felix gave up teaching and the family moved to Ascot Vale where the Offmans ran a milk bar.

'My name is Felix, but call me Fred,' became Offman's standard greeting when customers entered. It was about this time that he stopped playing music. Mimi recalls his moodiness and outbursts of anger, upending the table and sending dishes flying, and his growing obsession with betting.

Mimi's sense of her father oscillates. He was remote. She respected him. He was a strict disciplinarian. She loved him. She was afraid of him. She was close to him, but he rarely spoke to her. Her twin sister Sonia, I find out later, recalls a little more: of once coming upon Felix playing violin, alone, lost in his performing; of their home in Beirut, a large house with a veranda; of being wheeled in a pram by the beachside and across a boulevard lined with palm trees. Good times. But she too was wary of her father's temper.

What does Mimi know of the ancestors? Felix had four brothers and two sisters in Poland. The sisters were married and had children of their own. Felix had performed in a band. Or was it an orchestra? Felix and Julia wanted to return to Lodz in 1937 to show off their infant son, but the news was not good. The clouds of war were looming. It was too dangerous to risk the journey.

Felix never spoke of his internment in Aleppo. Or was it Beirut? It was during the war. Or was it later? He never talked about the past. Julia had mentioned it. He was separated from his family and held for over a year. Or was it seven months? That's all Mimi recalls. Her parents never explained it. Or perhaps she does not remember. The matter remains veiled in mystery, a black hole in the Offmans' Middle East sojourn. She does know that when the war ended Felix learned that his parents and siblings had perished in Auschwitz.

There are two objects that may throw more light on the story, Mimi says, as an afterthought. She retrieves two framed pieces from the wall and places them on the table. The smaller frame encloses a business card. Felix Offman's name is printed in Arabic and English, his vocation listed as *saxophoniste*. The larger frame encloses an A4-sized sheet of business stationery. In the top left-hand corner is a passport-sized shot of Felix, captioned 'Chef D'Orchestra, F. Offman'. The letterhead reads, 'Felo and his Swingers, Baghdad, 21/3/1938'.

This last shard of information arrests me. I have found the point the storyteller yearns for, the moment a tale yields its symmetry and attains an unexpected harmony. Mr Offman, my violin teacher, who had led me via a circuitous route to Naji Cohen, had lived and performed in Baghdad at about the same time that Naji had stopped beneath the balcony, transfixed by the playing of Blind Jamil. Perhaps all stories if pursued will eventually yield their symmetries, their unexpected meanings.

Then again, perhaps this is the storyteller's illusion, an innate longing to make sense of life's fragility and chaos, to contrive order out of what is in reality a play of chance. Does it matter? Perhaps it is enough to tell the story.

There is one other vital fragment in Mr Offman's story, an observation made by Rose, his daughter-in-law. Just months before his death in 2008, from Parkinson's disease, Sam Offman was on weekend leave from a nursing home. His movement was severely restricted. He could no longer play the violin or piano, yet music remained his great passion.

That Saturday afternoon he was lying on a couch in the living room, while his son Arieh was in the kitchen. Sam turned to his wife and said, 'Rosie, get my father's violin.'

'The violin?' Rose replied. 'You can't even hold a fork.'

'Bring me the violin.' Sam insisted.

She handed the encased instrument to him, and with great effort he squeezed it between his right leg and the back of the couch, to conceal it. It took five minutes to complete the task. When the case was finally in place he asked Rose to bring his son Arieh to him. An accomplished musician, Arieh plays violin, mandolin, clarinet, guitar and classical piano, and composes.

'Is there anything I can do for you?' he asked.

'No, but there is something I would like to give you,' Sam replied.

He reached down with shaking hands and grasped the case by the handle. With strenuous effort he lifted it and turned towards Arieh. 'Put your hands out,' he instructed.

'This is your grandfather's violin. It's the most precious thing I have of my father's. I know he would love you to have it, and I know he would love me to give it to you. He brought it with him from Lebanon. He played it with such finesse. I would like you to have it. I want you to have it now.'

The Dust of Life

In mid-January 1970, I arrived in Phnom Penh after a flight from Saigon. I rented a room in a travellers' hotel, but could not sit still. I was anxious to keep moving, as I had been for many weeks now.

I left my backpack on the floor and found my way down to the banks of the Tonle Sap River where a fisherman sat cross-legged mending his nets. Behind him, fishing boats swayed at their moorings beside thatched houses built over the shallows. I was taken by his unhurried movements, his quiet deliberation. He lifted his eyes as if all along he had been aware of my presence. I cannot recall how we spoke—perhaps in the broken French I owed to my high school studies—but I understood his invitation to accompany him that night to his fishing grounds.

With hours to spare before we were to set off, I walked along the river. As soon as I saw it, I knew I had found what I was looking for: a riverside teahouse, and a table with a view of the water. I started writing as soon as I was seated, spurred by a need to unburden myself of what I had witnessed in the past weeks in Vietnam.

Hours later, the lanterns in the teahouse had been lit and I was still writing, lost to a sequence of events that had begun when I boarded a plane in the southern Laotian city of Pakse bound for Saigon. We flew in a DC3, 'a collection of parts flying in loose formation' as it has been called, the nuts and bolts rattling, the engines grinding east over the border into South Vietnam.

The impact of the war, a certain kind of war, was soon apparent. In dried-up pockmarked paddies, and in swathes of field and forest scorched by chemical bombardment, trees denuded by defoliants, stripped of their bark just as napalm sears skin back to raw tissue. Blackened tracts of land were interspersed with surviving patches of forest, and somewhere beneath me I imagined them: Vietcong units moving in a network of tunnels, wielding machetes to cut through dense undergrowth and wading in the muddy waters of rice paddies, stalking the enemy, perhaps pausing to listen to the old workhorse of the air droning above them.

Nature itself was an enemy in this new era of warfare. The theory was simple. If the forests were removed, the guerillas would be denied their natural advantage.

The DC3 was rattling over a land where war had raged unabated for decades. This was my plan: to go in quickly, see the madness and get out before I incurred any damage. Twenty-year-olds in my country were subject to conscription and, since I could have been one of those conscripted if my birth date had come up in the lottery, I felt compelled to see it. At least, that was how I justified the journey, how I defined it. Only later did I begin to suspect there were other reasons for the venture.

Within hours of landing I was walking the streets of Saigon: a city of tree-lined boulevards, cathedrals and villas designed and built during decades of French occupation, now a ragged metropolis, overtaken by an under-class scavenging for survival, many in the service of troops on Rest and Recreation.

There was little sign of rest, but streets and alleys teeming with enterprises that flourish during times of war: black-market exchanges, bars and nightclubs tailored to the tastes of the occupying armies, hotels, from five star luxury to shabby hostels that doubled as bordellos. Never before had I seen so many people disfigured and crippled: maimed peasants and war veterans, men in wheelchairs, double amputees on improvised trolleys, invalids sitting in doorways and gutters, immobile, eyes barely flickering, staring at the flow of the city about them, at countless bicycles and trishaws careering between cars and trucks, motorbikes and military convoys.

'Watch your step, be vigilant, hold on to your bag or a passing motorcyclist will whip it off you before you fucking know it.' Always someone ready to offer advice to the novice.

At dusk people took to the roofs seeking relief from the heat and humidity. The shadows were lengthening, the night settling.

The city was pervaded by an uneasy sense of waiting. I slinked by, wary, having missed the curfew.

Military police patrolled in jeeps. The city was choked with the displaced, those uprooted by the fighting in provincial towns and villages. After curfew, some slept on the footpaths under makeshift shelters or out in the open. Entire families were huddled against walls, limbs intertwined, curled up and sleeping. Mangy dogs sniffed through the refuse. Couples lay face to face, smoking opium from elongated pipes that extended mouth to mouth between them. Children nestled against adults or lay alone, coiled within themselves like foetuses. Solitary individuals lay stretched out on their backs, staring at the heavens.

A cluster of men squatted over a card game in the shadows. Their listless eyes looked through me, longing for sleep, for oblivion. There was no way to enter this improvised city of phantoms and no way to shield myself from the odour of an abandoned humanity. In the morning they would be gone, dispersed across the city, an elusive army of survivors.

When at last I reached my destination, the house of the war correspondent who had invited me to stay with him, I banged on the door, and called out to the sleeping figure I could see through the barred windows. I knocked until I realised he was lost to a pill-induced stupor, to several hours of respite from the turmoil that was his daily reality.

'Hey, you want to see the war? Hop on board, mate. No worries. We don't have far to travel!' A big-hearted daredevil, more boy than man in appearance, he wore his naivety like an identification tag. He held fast to his persona, seeming to know instinctively that his air of innocence was what protected him.

We had met on my first day in Saigon and, over a drink, he'd told me that he had left Australia four years earlier at sixteen, and had journeyed overland with a thirst for adventure. As soon as he crossed the Thai border into Indochina he knew he had found his nirvana. Like so many, he had fallen for the allure of the live-for-the-day mentality and adrenaline rushes that war induces.

He rode his motorcycle from Vietnam to Laos to Cambodia and back as if there were no borders and no tomorrows, taking charcoal temple drawings into Saigon where he sold them as souvenirs to US soldiers. He had picked up languages and dialects with the keen ear of a guileless traveller and had worked as an interpreter. He felt an affinity with the people and now aspired to be a photojournalist.

I climbed aboard and rode behind him, buoyed by his confidence as he careered to the outskirts of the city and beyond, past munitions depots and bases, and mile upon mile of military hardware. A landscape of khaki and rust, the colours of occupation, relieved by clumps of palms, oases of monsoon greens, glimpses of rainforest.

All was rushing past, countryside blurring, farmers hauling produce by the side of road, military vehicles moving to and from the city. And we were singing, invigorated by a sense of invincibility, bumping over ruts and potholes, forgetting that out there life and death were dancing, the body count mounting.

The following day chance meetings led me to an apartment, a safe haven for US soldiers who were contemplating desertion. They sat cross-legged on the carpet and talked, as if in one voice, of their fears and uncertainties. They called the Vietcong 'Charlie', the slang name for the enemy. Or the more derogatory 'dink' or 'gook', and 'slant-eye' for good measure, names born of fear of the unfathomable other.

Their comrades, the soldiers told me, were using speed and cocaine, acid, dope, or plain beer and spirits, anything to alter or deaden the reality. It was the height of a war that had been fought far too long and had spawned far too many casualties, with no dividend. The men knew full well that back home the anti-war movement was gathering momentum, and that many who had once supported them were now growing weary of the fight. And they knew that if their luck ran out they would return as corpses, or as maimed pariahs.

They were grunts, the lowest on the rungs of the military hierarchy, foot soldiers, some still teenagers, their eyes shot through with fear and wonder, like animals mesmerised by spotlights, not knowing where to run, where to hide, where to find refuge. They had been shoved onto choppers, lowered into forest clearings, their bodies weighed down by military hardware, their faces painted for night battle. They had tramped through jungle and paddy and crawled through elephant grass, stinking of fear and swamp water.

Who can we trust, the eyes seemed to ask, who can we believe, who knows what is going on, who is profiting, who is being saved, who protected, who being conned or deluded? You cannot comprehend what we have seen, what we have endured, what we have been doing. You are not one of us. You are free to come and go, you lucky bastard. You have been spared the horror.

You have to be in it to know that war is literally shit, a chaos of rotting bowels, fevers and quagmires, infested with platoons of mosquitoes. You can't stop the infernal itch. You weep from wanting to be clean. You sprinkle powders, apply oils and ointments, yet still you can't cleanse yourself of the dirt, or get rid of the stench. We're going mad, the eyes told me, tipping into insanity.

We did not bargain on seeing things that will haunt us forever: the shredded bodies of comrades, the corpses of nameless enemies, and the fear and suspicion in the eyes of the villagers we thought we were protecting. This is why we are holed up in this apartment, in hiding, waiting for an escape from the death and disfigurement that stalks us. So now we roll joints and pass them from one to the other. There is always one on the go, brother. You are welcome to join us.

They inhaled deeply, filled the room with their smoke, and obsessed over the morbid details, Vietcong landmines that activated as soon as the unsuspecting foot was lifted, mines that bounced chest height with shrapnel, mines that exploded horizontally, tearing apart the lower body. The talk followed the route of the joint, one voice coalescing into the next, until there was little distinction between one and the other.

'It's a fucking lottery, brother. One false move and then the medics save what is left of you,' said one voice. 'Then they ship you home with a pension to replace your legs, and a fucking medal to replace your penis,' said a second. 'To a country where no one wants to know you,' added a third.

'And not even here are we safe, hidden away in the city. Charlie is everywhere. Charlie is in the street. Charlie is the rickshaw driver, the waiter serving behind the bar counter. Charlie is the gook slinking by in a hat posing as a peasant, a street vendor. Charlie is the dink eyeing you wherever you go. Charlie is on the take with one hand reaching for your wallet, and the other itching to kill you. Charlie is everywhere, watching, waiting.'

Of my many encounters in Saigon, there is one that most haunted me. An American correspondent, distressed by what he had witnessed, had set up a refuge for street boys. A loose arrangement as I recall it: rooms strewn with straw mats, wicker chairs, sleeping bags and blankets.

The boys, dressed in shorts and short-sleeved shirts, ranging in age from perhaps seven to seventeen, roamed Saigon in thongs or bare-footed, doing business with allied soldiers in their fast-talking street spiel: 'You want something, man? You want shoeshine? You want dirty picture? You want tailor make shirt? Hey man, you want woman, number one girl, very soft, very beautiful?'

In between missions they gathered in the refuge, played cards, boasted of their exploits, schemed and argued, shared trade secrets and contacts, and slept. I observed them late one night, sprawled on their mats in random postures, stretched out, curled up, filling out the room with their restless movements. *Bui doi,* the boys were called, 'the dust of life', but in this moment of blessed sleep they were a brotherhood united by common circumstance, living a semblance of family life in a transient haven in a warring city where the bonds of civility had been strained beyond the limits.

A boy of fifteen, one of the residents of the refuge, his watchful eyes darting about, taking in everything, guided me through the streets of Cholon, the Chinese quarter, towards the Saigon River. Finely attuned to the streets, he walked with a swagger, chest puffed out in exaggerated machismo.

He led me past buildings fractured and bullet marked, evidence of the fierce fighting two years earlier when the Vietcong rose up in a frenzied attack that came to be known as the Tet Offensive. We walked past pizzerias, kerbside eateries, flower stalls, street markets, and through alleys where deserters in pith helmets and peaked caps traded in US Army supplies; past bars that catered to every taste, every persuasion, of the occupying armies. Grunts leaned on jukeboxes drawling country and western, Johnny Cash and Elvis, *Are you lonesome tonight. Will you still love me tomorrow?* Doris Day crooning *My heart longs for the black hills, the black hills of Dakota,* the Rolling Stones intoning *You can't always get what you want,* and the grunts singing along in unison, as if responding to the lead of a Baptist preacher.

In bars for blacks, brothers greeted each other with 'dap' handshakes and jived to gospel and Motown songs that were taking on new meanings. Ben E. King performing *There is a rose in Spanish Harlem,* John Lee Hooker strumming the 'Hobo Blues', Odetta singing *Sometimes I feel like a motherless child,* Jimi

Hendrix obliterating fear and loathing with manic electric guitar riffs. The black grunts were figuring it out, thinking it through, and asking questions: why are we stuck in this hellhole fighting Charlie when, come to think of it, no Charlie ever called me honky, no Vietcong ever called me nigger?

Vietnamese songs flowed from eating houses, from roadside stalls and from transistors dangling on handlebars, accompanied by the smell of frying food, of incense and camphor smoke, the chime of temple bells and the incessant drone of the traffic. And there were moments of grace: a girl running from an alley, exuberant, trailing a kite made of newspaper. The kite soared then fell. The girl bent over to recover it. The kite lifted, struggled and, regaining momentum, rose above the rooftops. A boy on crutches, leg amputated above the knee, dribbled a soccer ball with his intact leg, frowning in concentration.

Girls played jacks on the pavement; women plucked chickens and hauled water, gossiping, getting on with the business of living. A woman sat on a wooden stool on the pavement, oblivious to the chaos around her, stroking the hair of a grandchild, picking through the scalp in search of vermin. Woks glistened with slices of fish jumping about on hot oil like frogs leaping in and out of the sunlight.

The boy took me into an eating house. He grinned at the cooks and waiters and the scantily clad waitresses, and strutted about like a seasoned performer. Once seated, he drew out a wad of tobacco and a tin containing squares of newspaper. He laid them on the table and worked methodically. I had never seen anyone roll a cigarette with such speed and dexterity. One flick of the wrist and he was settling back, puffing like a veteran, straining his voice above the tumult to recount a story in the serviceable English he had acquired in his dealings with the occupying army.

He spoke without emotion, pausing to inhale and then blow smoke rings, following their progress with his eyes, but always on the lookout, guided by instinct, the imperatives of survival. His face was alternately young and ancient, of a boy cynical before his time, but a boy nevertheless. Come to think of it, he was not much younger than the grunts I had smoked with a night earlier.

Two years ago his village was bombed, he said, pausing to puff, to wave to an acquaintance making his way past the table. I strained to make out his tumble of words, the rapid-fire patois propelled by youthful bravado. The village was on fire, he seemed to be saying, and he was running from the flames, sprinting to the edge of the forest, stopping at the trees to look back at the ducks and pigs scattering, water buffalos bellowing, horses screaming, and houses exploding, his one of them.

He talked so fast the images seemed to trip over each other. One moment the house was there in full view—the thatched roof, the doorway to his homecomings—and the next, it was turning to blacks and greys, reducing to the hues of a photographic negative, breaking down into cinders and ashes.

The boy, pausing, looked back long enough to know that he would never again see his parents among the living. They had become, as would one day be revealed, two of the millions of Indochinese killed, displaced and wounded within a decade, the great majority of whom were rice growers, handlers of livestock, tenders of orchards and market gardens, carers of children. Civilian fodder caught in the crossfire.

And as he talked, I was transported back ten years and thousands of kilometres to a single-fronted Victorian terrace in an inner Melbourne suburb. Late at night woken by my mother crying out Mama! Mama! It happened more than once, this dream accompanied by the cry of Mama! Mama!

One night I crept from my bedroom along the linoleum passage, and stopped by the door of the front bedroom, straining to listen to my mother's urgent Yiddish whispering as she told my father of a village on fire and her running from the flames with her brothers and sisters as, one by one, they fell, leaving her the only one running.

Her dream echoed the stories told by the ex-partisan who regularly came to the house to reminisce with my parents about their shared past on the borderlands of eastern Poland and his exploits in the forests as a fighter. He talked of the ambush that had claimed his comrades, how he had run, legs bleeding from bullet wounds, driven beyond pain and panic by a desperate will to survive. And to prove his point, he had lifted the cuffs of his trousers, allowing us to see the scars that ran like ploughed furrows beside his shinbones.

This is how war appeared in my youthful imagination: a chaos of ambushes and burning forests, buildings exploding, a constant running and dodging, thoroughfares clogged with people, horse-drawn carts laden with belongings, planes diving low, randomly strafing men, women and children fleeing in collective panic. The images became a part of my being, contained within that overarching memory of my mother recounting her dream of horror.

The burning village could have been her slum neighbourhood in the city of Bialystok where she spent much of her childhood. It could have been Bransk or Grodek, Bielsk, Orly, or any one of the towns and hamlets in the borderlands of Russia and Poland where her ancestors had lived for half a millennium.

In time her dreams entered mine, spawning my own recurring dream of a forest clearing enclosed by trees behind which I hid with my older brother, the two of us gazing in terror as bodies were cast into the flames by sinister figures. The dream invariably ended with the flames lighting up our faces, both of us being discovered, and the figures advancing towards us.

I had been brought up on tales of war and its brutalities, had absorbed them from memorial albums that were compiled postwar by survivors as an act of homage and restoration. 'Memory books', they were called, each one dedicated to a particular city, town or village, with bilingual texts in Yiddish and English, and photos of the time before their destruction, of characters and institutions, streets and buildings, familiar landmarks. And accounts of their obliteration, with the names of each victim, and images of mass deportation, sites of slaughter, entire neighbourhoods reduced to rubble.

Perhaps this legacy was why I had embarked upon my journey to this war-torn country. No one had ordered me to go. No uniform bound me. No one even knew I had undertaken the journey. I needed to see it for myself. And now that I had been there, and had seen the mayhem and horror, I needed to get it out on paper, to expunge it.

Yet there was something else, a feeling of unease that I first sensed when riding pillion passenger behind the young adventurer, carried along by his energy and captive to the paradox: the allure of war despite the horror, the exhilarating danger that drew some correspondents back into the fray, like addicts. They no longer knew whether they were witness or voyeur, critic or accomplice. I felt that unease again on my post-curfew walk, past the makeshift pavement shanties. I was an outsider after all, an intruder into a community bound by misery, moving by in the shadows.

And just days later, I was out and about in Phnom Penh, free to sit as I now did at a window table by the Tonle Sap River, at liberty to move around or to leave, unlike the haunted grunts gone AWOL, unlike the people of Saigon moving about an occupied city, and unlike the 'dust of life', that brotherhood of street boys.

I felt uneasy too at the memory of the boy who had given me his story. He had recounted it with bravado and abandon, his voice barely rising above the din of competing voices, whirring fans and the clutter of dishes. And when the meal was over, in a gesture that brooked no protest, he had insisted he pay. He pulled out a wallet, and shelled out the notes with a flourish, leaving a tip for good measure.

I left the Phnom Penh teahouse well after nightfall, returning to the riverbank and that enclave of houses above the water, where, as prearranged, I met the fisherman. He untied the ropes and rowed out. One hundred metres from the banks he started the outboard motor and put-putted to the confluence of two massive waterways, the Tonle Sap and the Mekong. He cut the engine, laid out the nets and, when he was done, settled back with a cigarette.

The night was given over to the faint hoot of steamers and barges, the distant lights of the city. The fisherman heated a pot of rice, fish and vegetables over a primus stove. And when we had finished eating, he took out a bamboo flute and leaned back against the canvas shelter.

The notes were hesitant at first, as if waking from slumber. The fisherman's eyes were fixed on the water, the rhythm of his playing dictated by the boat's movements. In time, the distinction between flute and water, bamboo and breeze vanished, and all that remained was the flow of the notes—a melody that belonged to streams and rivers, outside and beyond history, beyond the scourge of contending armies, beyond the stench of camps and shantytowns housing the displaced and exiled. Beyond the madness.

Within months of my visit, the city that glittered on the shores was plunged into chaos, the river laid to siege, cutting off Phnom Penh's lifeline. To navigate its waters beyond the city's limits was fatal. Rebels roamed the banks and lay in ambush within striking distance.

On April 17 1975, after years of intermittent siege, the city fell to the Khmer Rouge. In an act of ideologically fuelled brutality the two and a half million residents were driven into the countryside. Phnom Penh was emptied.

The city became a ghostly no-man's-land, the country a killing field. More than one and a half million Cambodians died, and many thousands fled for their lives, stealing across stretches of rice paddy and forest littered with mines and booby traps, to stagnate for years on end in borderland camps and makeshift villages.

And many times, I have wondered what happened to that fisherman, to his livelihood, his village, his nightly forays upon the river. To his song.

Bella Ciao

Monsieur and Madame owned a café and motel on the Rue du Lac between Lausanne and Geneva. Madame managed the motel, and Monsieur the apple orchards and vineyards on the slopes above Lake Geneva. Each year they hired foreign workers to bring in the harvest, and each year a group of twenty women travelled there from their hometown in Italy.

The women worked seven days a week, sunrise to dusk, for three months, and in the autumn of 1973 I worked alongside them. They smelled of earth and spices, and took good care of their appearance. They rose in the pre-dawn dark, applied powder and lipstick, and ate a hasty breakfast before hoisting themselves into the tray of the truck that ferried them from the highway over unpaved pathways to the orchards.

The eldest was Asunta, a matriarch of sixty-eight. Her hair was a frizzy mass of grey, her skin tough and darkened. Her ample body was swathed in layers of skirts and jumpers. She walked with a slow rolling gait, weighed down by her age. Yet a zest for life radiated from her eyes. 'Our men are useless,' she laughed. 'We have to leave them behind to go and make a living.'

'We are glad to be rid of them for a while,' said Martina, at forty-eight the youngest. 'We do not have to endure them pestering us for our bodies, and do not have to push them off with our excuses. Besides, what work is there back home except for the few lira we make from our exhausted farmlands?' A Marlene Dietrich lookalike, her hair was dyed blonde, her fingernails freshly painted, her pale blue-green eyes accentuated by mascara. She moved with elegance, protective of the vestiges of her youth, her enduring beauty.

When the day was done the women were driven back to the workers' quarters where they remained on call to clean the round-the-clock café, since Madame was obsessed with cleanliness and determined that all would be in perfect order, scoured and dusted, swabbed and polished. Alas the effect was a sickly smell of antiseptic in the café and the motel corridors.

In the evening the women fussed over me in their quarters as if I were a lost son returned after years of absence. The kitchen common room was criss-crossed by cords pegged with massive bloomers, sweaters and cardigans, bras, petticoats, skirts and stockings. We ate and drank and warmed ourselves by the stove, and talked in the pidgin German the women had acquired during years of war and occupation.

Our conversations continued out in the orchards when Thomas, the head foreman, was away on an errand. As soon as the groan of the truck faded we descended the ladders and gathered fallen twigs and branches. We lit a fire and, as on the previous evening, passed round a flask of grappa, almond biscuits and slices of cheese and salami that the women carried in hidden recesses of their clothing.

Issen the Kosovo Albanian—cigarette stuck at the corner of his lips—resumed his boasts about his semen, which he claimed had the power to penetrate doors and shatter windows. It would take flight, he asserted, over mountain slopes and rivers towards distant countries, bypassing borders. With each telling his prowess expanded, and soon his semen was soaring at the speed of light, hurtling over continents and oceans.

Not to be denied, Idir the boyish Moroccan chimed in with virginal boasts of his conquests. The number grew with each boast until he was lord and master of an entire harem. Gil, the ageing Spaniard, face stained with red blotches, grasped the flask, gulped down more than his fill and ran excitedly in circles at the sound of an aeroplane approaching. He raised his face and shot up his arm in a fascist salute exclaiming, 'Luftwaffe! Luftwaffe!' Incensed, Miro the Yugoslav hummed German beer hall ditties, acquired during work stints in Hamburg, interspersed with snatches of the *Internationale*.

So it went: the grappa and cheese, boasts and gossip, Gil leering over Martina who kept him at bay with contemptuous glances, the laughter building towards hysteria, until all was abruptly ended by the distant groan of the truck returning. The men pissed on the fire and stamped out the embers. We scurried up the ladders and resumed picking well before the truck arrived in the clearing.

Paolo was a guest worker from Italy. A heavyset man, he wore a navy blue cap and woollen jacket and his overalls tucked into knee-high gumboots. His movements were slow and deliberate, his tired gaze leavened by a fixed smile, but rarely a grimace. He was too shy and generous for that.

He worked three jobs, and trudged from one to the other in a state of weariness: from his ten-hour days as a farmhand in Monsieur's groves and vineyards to weekend evening stints as a taxi driver, and nightly shifts in a bottle-making factory supervising workers on the assembly lines.

I accompanied him one night to his workplace, where he proudly took me on a tour of the factory. Behold my domain, his eyes were saying, behold my charges. Rows of women dressed in overalls sat at conveyor belts, their eyes fixed on the passing bottles, mesmerised. When a woman detected a flaw she picked out the offending bottle and hurled it over her shoulder, where it crashed into bins to be crushed and recycled.

Nothing wasted or discarded. Night after night the drone of the belt, the robotic movements, the hypnotic allure of the passing bottles. The shift workers moved about a nocturnal zone separated from the outside world, from normal living.

I left Paolo and set out on the Rue du Lac for the drive back to the workers' quarters. On the upper slopes, the orchards we tended by day were lost to the darkness. I wound down the window and sucked in the night air. And six hours later the alarm was ringing, drawing me out of bed into the dawn where Paolo was back on board the truck as if no time had passed since I last saw him.

Sitting beside him, cigarette glued to his mouth, Issen stared vacantly into the distance. Gil sprawled between us, blinking away his hangover. Idir and Miro dozed side by side, as if they had been carted out from their beds and deposited where they lay, still sleeping. The women were arranging themselves on makeshift cushions made up of blankets and hessian sacking, preparing themselves for the journey. And Thomas, the benevolent blue-eyed foreman, in his customary blue overalls, was at the wheel humming, *The sky is blue, the sun shines too, deep in the heart of Texas,* singing to impress me, the English speaker, with one line of the lyrics of one song, which he sang over and over.

His face was set in a cheerful grin as the truck ascended. The mountain air recharged us, and through the mists emerged a battalion of Swiss soldiers on military exercises. They crept in a half crouch through vineyards, followed by a column of tanks and armoured vehicles, on the alert for phantom enemies. 'There goes the might of the Swiss army,' said Miro, 'God help us.' 'Luftwaffe. Luftwaffe,' mumbled Gil, his arm outstretched, shaking with delirium tremens.

Within the hour we were at work, the older women on the ground, reaching up to pick the apples, the younger workers scaling the ladders, leaning into the foliage. Paolo followed in our wake with a saw and secateurs. He placed a ladder against the trees that had been picked, steadying it to make sure of his safety before climbing it with measured steps and settling on an upper rung, where he set about pruning the branches with the resigned air of a draught horse.

So it continued, day after day, dawn to dusk, week after week. Autumn was giving way to winter. The first snows were falling, the picking season was coming to an end, and Thomas was away on an errand. We lit a fire, passed round the grappa, and stamped our feet to keep warm while the fire was building. And, as if responding to an innate signal, the voices of the women began rising—a makeshift choir finding its way to the melody and, finally, the lyrics:

One morning when I awakened
O bella, ciao! Bella, ciao! Bella, ciao, ciao, ciao!
One morning when I awakened
I found invaders all around

Oh partisan, come take me with you
O bella, ciao! Bella, ciao! Bella, ciao, ciao, ciao!
Oh partisan, come take me with you
Because I feel ready to die

If I die fighting as a partisan
O bella, ciao! Bella, ciao! Bella, ciao, ciao, ciao!
If I die fighting as a partisan
You must come and bury me.

To this day I remember the expressions on the women's faces: the knowing eye, the acute sharpness, tempered by a glint of mischief, a touch of radiance. The women had been steeled during the war in mountain hideouts, and on clandestine missions as partisans in the anti-fascist resistance. They were at ease with the physical world, their feet firmly planted on the earth, an anchor to their yearning. They moved through their days step by step like slow whirling dervishes, biding their time, conserving energy, and by nightfall they were on the truck for the journey back to the workers' quarters.

A blessed weariness descended. The women huddled together, murmuring in conversation. Gil and Idir were dozing, Miro and Issen lying back in silence, cigarette butts glowing, and Paolo was seated between them, holding his knees to his chest, staring blankly. The moon had broken clear, and seemed so close we were tempted to reach up and touch it. We lay back on the tray, our eyes diverted by a flock of birds in V-formation embarking on their annual migrations.

This is who they were, the men and women I worked with, migrating birds bound to seasonal cycles of farewells and arrivals, departures and return journeys. I envisaged them setting out from their homes on foot or wagons, by bus or train, barely glancing back, emotions kept in check, eyes firmly on the horizon, the faces of loved ones vanishing, their barren farmlands receding. Their movement punctuated by frontier crossings, customs inspections, dusty bus depots, drab waiting rooms and way-stops at cheap cafés. While at each border, the fear of rejection.

There was no romance in the guest workers' lives, but the

austerity of cheap lodgings and barracks, and the chronic ache of extended absences, relieved by wine, an idle boast, a hit of caffeine. The incessant movement to and from orchard and factory, building site and vineyard, mines and quarries, to and from the homes that they cleaned or lived in as domestics. And when the stint was done, back to their homelands laden with cash and presents, and a sense of worldliness from having journeyed to foreign places. Then, in time, back on the road and a renewal of the migratory cycle.

As we drove back to the workers' quarters, not even the jolts could rouse the bodies sprawled beside me. While in the cabin, like a broken record, his voice barely audible above the din of the motor, Thomas was crooning, *The sky is blue, the shine shines too, deep in the heart of Texas.*

The sky was blue, the sun shone too, the harvest was all but over, but all was not well. Posters had appeared overnight. In Geneva and Lausanne, in towns and mountain hamlets, on walls and lampposts and makeshift billboards. Invisible forces were on the move, hit-and-run brigades propagating their opposing messages.

A public argument had broken out in Switzerland in the winter of 1973. A global oil crisis was threatening recession, adding weight to a perennial suspicion. A referendum was imminent, the question formulated: Yes or no? Should guest workers be allowed in the country? 'They are creeping in by the back door, diluting our culture, taking our jobs when we need them. They are stealing in while we sleep, crossing our borders, engaging in shady doings, amassing secret fortunes,' argued the naysayers.

'They grow our economies, relieve labour shortages, provide a market for our products, domestics for our families, nannies for our children, labour for our sewers and abattoirs,' countered the supporters, reinforcing their case with photos of cleaners, factory hands, garbage collectors and farm workers, holding crowbars and shovels, brooms and hammers. 'Would you want to do such jobs?' read the captions.

Monsieur's workers barely glanced at the posters. They had seen it all before, and had heard the predictable arguments. Let them fight it out, they indicated with their grimaces. Whichever way it goes, we have no say in it. All we can do is take our chances.

Only Issen responded. He stood up and lurched on the back of the moving truck like a drunken seaman. He steadied himself against the back of the cabin, cigarette between his lips as if it were a natural extension of his body. And with one hand held against the cabin, he moved the other to and fro, in front of his crotch.

'My semen is so strong it can take out the posters in one hit,' he boasted, thrusting his pelvis towards the posters of the naysayers, his eyes following the imagined trajectory to its target. And for once, his workmates cheered him, and dissolved into laughter as they mimicked his actions.

The final task of the season was to gather the fruit scattered over the snow. The fallen apples were to be used in making schnapps. The women bent down to gather the fruit into picking aprons. They emptied the apples into wooden boxes that Issen and I carried to the moving tractor driven by Paolo.

With each successive row the tractor moved faster. The women rose to their knees, emptied their picking aprons and turned back to the snow. Martina led the way. She possessed an agility that enabled her to bend over with seeming ease despite the bulk of her winter clothing, but old Asunta had great difficulty. She crawled on her hands and knees short of breath, determined not to fall too far behind her companions.

I pleaded with Paulo to slow down. He turned, shrugged his shoulders and continued to drive, oblivious to my bleating. Asunta struggled to her feet and pulled me aside with a hint of annoyance: 'This will not help us,' she said. 'Paolo is no different. If he slows down he will lose his job and we will lose ours. He is only doing what he must. This is how it is.'

She lowered herself back onto her hands and knees and continued. Moments later, she began humming. One by one the women took up her lead, reinforcing her barely audible singing:

Bury me there, up in the mountains
O bella, ciao! Bella, ciao! Bella, ciao, ciao, ciao!
Bury me up there in the mountains
Shade my grave with a lovely flower

So all the people who pass that way
O bella, ciao! Bella, ciao! Bella, ciao, ciao, ciao!
So all the people who pass that way
Will say 'Oh see that lovely flower!'

'Ah that's the flower of the partisan fighter'
O bella, ciao! Bella, ciao! Bella, ciao, ciao, ciao!
'Ah that's the flower of the partisan fighter
Who died for freedom's sake!'

The pace of the tractor did not slow, but Paolo too was mouthing the words. He clung to the wheel with his eyes fixed on the track, a tenacious peasant with a stoic grimace. I watched the women working over the snow-flecked earth. Beyond the tree line, the mountain was lost in the mists and, far below, the lake, a grey sheet beneath a feeble sun, was barely glistening.

I looked back towards Asunta and, sensing my presence, she lifted her head and winked. Then she turned her face back to the earth and scrambled over the melting sludge, clawing apples into her picking apron. And with renewed vigour, continued singing.

The Music Box

The village lies near the border. I say lies, for here on the flat-lands of eastern Poland time sleeps. In the autumn of 1986, address in hand, I walked from the station along the railway embankment. A teenage boy idled by the tracks scanning the horizon. He picked up a handful of stones and cast them at the rails, one by one, delighting in the resonant ping when one hit its target.

Like a hare detecting a movement, he cocked his head and stared into the distance. For a time the approaching train seemed to move slowly, then it was upon us, playing havoc with the silence. Passengers' faces flitted by, leaving a yearning for distant places.

I showed the boy the address and he led the way along a clay pathway. Coiled bales of hay were lined up in neat rows in recently cut paddocks. Birch and conifers fringed the farmlands. Peasants, bent over double, harvested potatoes and turnips. A farmer, rope tethered round his shoulders, worked a horse-drawn plough. The horse's flanks were damp with sweat, its nostrils flaring. The onion-shaped domes of a church glinted in the distance.

The path broke off from the embankment and twenty minutes later we were in the village. The boy took me to the house and vanished.

The shutters were open and fastened against the weatherboard. Sunflowers stood in a vase on the windowsill. A cat lay outstretched on a table behind the window. It sat up and eyed my progress to the front door.

Though we had never met, Katrina welcomed me warmly. Stylishly dressed in a white blouse, a tight-waisted black skirt, high heels and sheer nylon stockings, she wore makeup and her nails were varnished. Beside her, like a faithful valet, stood her fifteen-year-old son, Stefan. His complexion was pale, his shoulders slightly stooped, and beneath his eyes the light-blue pallor of late nights of study.

I passed on regards to Katrina from a friend of hers I had met in Bialystok, and handed her the envelope I had offered to deliver. We spoke in a mixture of French, English and German. Though her fluency was impressive in all three, certainly far better than mine in French and German, she expressed frustration at her lack of command of the languages.

From the outside, the house was like the others in the village, a variation of brightly painted weatherboard, but inside, in sharp contrast to the homes I had entered in nearby towns and hamlets, the floorboards were polished and there were books scattered over the tables, the shelves and sofas and stacked upon the mantelpiece: volumes in Polish and French, Russian, English and German. Katrina spent her days reading between her household duties. Her interests ranged from history and philosophy to literary journals and novels.

She spoke quickly, as if anxious to impress on me her sense of taste, and her passions. There was urgency in her short, hurried steps and her emphatic hand gestures. At her insistence Stefan showed me his stamp collection. We sat side by side on a sofa as Stefan navigated the pages of his albums. He travelled from country to country with the ease of a mariner who had many times undertaken the journey.

When we were done, we leaned over an atlas and I traced the circuitous route I had taken from Melbourne, via Beijing, across Siberia, the length of the Soviet Empire and, after a change of trains in Moscow, southwest to Warsaw, then back east to the borderland towns and villages of my ancestors. And finally, following a chance encounter in the city of Bialystok, to this hamlet, and the timber house where Stefan and I sat over maps like plotting conspirators.

Katrina unlocked a drawer and took out a pile of letters. The envelopes bore stamps from Britain, France and West Germany. In time she would allow Stefan to steam them off for his collection. They were treasured possessions, letters from friends abroad, her lifeline to what she imagined was a world of refinement and freedom. Mother and son were partners in their infatuation with other places.

As the afternoon progressed they became expectant. Nervous. They glanced at each other, towards the door and at their watches. Katrina's husband, Tomas, was due home at any moment. He might arrive drunk, or in a dark mood. With luck he would be sober. Though he was not yet in sight Katrina and Stefan spoke of him in a near whisper.

At the sound of a vehicle pulling up Stefan announced his father's arrival. Through the window could be seen a battered truck. The tyres were muddy and the windscreen was splattered with the remains of insects. On the tray lay two ladders, a chainsaw and sawn logs and branches.

A tall, broad-shouldered man, Tomas stooped low beneath the lintel. He had returned from an overnight sojourn in the Bialowieza Forest, a vast nature reserve straddling the eastern border. His face and arms were sun-beaten. His body was muscular and heavy, and his clothes smelt of damp and resin. He addressed his wife as 'mother' and shook my hands in greeting. He took a bottle of champagne from the drinks cabinet and handed it to me with childish pleasure. He was the man of the house, the host, and this was French champagne, he proudly indicated, pointing to the label.

Katrina and Stefan stood to the side as he poured the champagne into crystal glasses. Without a word Tomas picked up a carved silver music box from the mantelpiece. He handled it gently, carefully placing it down on the table. It was a present he had bought for his wife when he was a guest worker in Switzerland.

He glanced nervously at Katrina as he set it in motion, but

she looked away. The song, the theme from the film *Love Story*, her contemptuous expression indicated, was beneath her. It was her measure of the man, his lack of refinement and his cheap sentimentality. With each glance from her husband Katrina withdrew further. In his presence she seemed much smaller, but still defiant.

Tomas put his hand to his forehead. He was floundering. The polished floorboards were at sharp odds with his heavy work boots. He looked at the books and pamphlets as if he did not recognise his surroundings. With great effort he tried to regain the awkward grin he had worn when he entered.

I had unwittingly stepped into a domestic drama. I could not know the details or nuances. I had no idea of the history, of what had once brought husband and wife together and the chain of events that had drawn them apart. Perhaps there had been outbursts of rage, bouts of violence, chronic drunkenness, or misunderstandings that had compounded into an irretrievable breakdown. All I had was what I sensed before me in that cottage in an isolated village in the shadows of nightfall.

Husband and wife were locked from each other. At least, this is how I saw it. They had devised separate exits for their torment, he through drink and solitary sojourns in the forests, she through dreams of starting anew in the West. Theirs was just one tiny drama in the vast expanses of the Soviet empire and its satellite nations. They were trapped in a moment of history, enclosed behind the Iron Curtain.

He was of the forest and silences, night fires and shadows, conifers and the aroma of resin. He yearned for romance, she for salons and theatres, elevated conversation, the classical and the elegant. She longed for nocturnes and concertos, he for a simple love song. And I was just passing through.

After dinner Tomas slept on a sofa while Stefan sat at a table studying. The shutters were closed; the sunflowers drooped. The cat lay asleep at Katrina's feet while she sat on a couch, reading. The house was silent, save for the ticking of a grandfather clock and its hourly tolling. It stood in a corner beside a precarious tower of books, a breath away from toppling.

Assuring me that Stefan was beyond rousing, Katrina and Stefan ushered me out of the house for a walk through the village. The domes of the church were silhouetted against the night sky. Many houses were dark, their inhabitants retired for the night. On the roadside stood a shrine to the Madonna, and at the base lay a wilted posy of flowers. Beyond the street, the village gave way to darkness.

Our footsteps triggered a chorus of barks and howls. Katrina and Stefan paid no attention. They walked without looking about them. Their minds were firmly on their purpose, and Katrina was imploring, 'Can you help us? Please, can you arrange for us a visa? If we do not get out soon, our lives will be wasted. We need a sponsor, permits. Help us leave this black hole. We are choking.'

Hours later I lay awake on the sofa bed. Katrina, Stefan and Tomas were sleeping. In the morning I would continue my journey, and tomorrow night I would be elsewhere. I was travelling alone, and this is how I preferred it. I was free to come as I pleased, to enter into other people's lives, and move on when it suited me. And free to rise now from my bed at the sound of hooves and the creaking of wheels over the roadway.

I pushed open the shutters. A horse-drawn cart, piled high with bales of hay was passing. The farmer was leading the horse, walking slowly before it. I watched the cart until it vanished, then glanced back at Tomas who lay asleep, his legs curled in a foetal position to fit the sofa.

Yes, I was just passing through. Or was I? This journey was different from those I had previously undertaken. I was deep in my ancestral territory, and had been for more than six weeks now. On nights like this my forebears had slept in the settlements of these borderlands, perhaps in this very village. Yet it had ended badly. My perception was affected by what I knew, coloured a shade darker. A generation had been wiped out, and those few who remained had emigrated. I glanced at the table. The music box glinted: a brittle presence in the near darkness.

When I awoke, Tomas was fully dressed and waiting. I had planned to move on by train, but he insisted on taking me with him. I was his guest. Why go by train if he could give me a lift, he argued. The truck was ready, the sandwiches packed. Besides, the Bialowieza Forest, my intended destination, was his workplace. To refuse would be a slight upon his hospitality.

Katrina had yet to put on her makeup. She appeared older, deflated. The slight greying in the temples was now visible. Instead of high heels, she was wearing slippers. She was long up, and had prepared breakfast. The urgency of the previous night had evaporated.

Mother and son were silent. Their mood had shifted in tandem to resignation and sullen defiance. They saw me to the door, shook my hand, and stood on the doorstep, listlessly. They barely waved as Tomas backed onto the roadway. They knew as well as I did that I would not help them.

Tomas drove to the end of the street and stopped in front of a wooden cottage. It was smaller than the one we had just left, a doll's house. The dark green paint on the wood shutters was flaking. An old woman seated at a table could be seen through the window.

She was by the door to greet us by the time we arrived, a short and stout woman, white hair tied back in a simple bun. Tomas bent over to kiss her on the forehead. She insisted on serving breakfast despite my protests. Her face was fixed with the weary smile of those who have fulfilled life's tasks and are quietly waiting. She walked slowly about the kitchen and spoke in a childish whisper.

On the table by the window were two potted geraniums and a biscuit tin overflowing with sewing needles, tape measures and reels of cotton. Beside the tin lay the dress she had been mending. Just one book was visible, the Bible. It sat on the mantelpiece beside a plaster statuette of Jesus on the cross, trapped in his agony. On the wall hung a framed poster of the Madonna, hand on heart, eyelids lowered.

The house was considerably smaller than Tomas's, the carpets threadbare. Embroidered pillows lay scattered over the aged sofas and armchairs. The furniture, the wood stove, the cushions and tablecloth brought to mind ageing comfort. The one object the two houses had in common was the grandfather clock. Here it stood against the living-room wall. The clock was at home here, as was Tomas. Though few words passed between them, there was an intimacy between mother and son that was absent between wife and husband.

By the time we returned to the truck, Tomas's mother was back at her post by the table, gazing out blankly. She was a still life, beyond haste, beyond hoping. I could only guess at what she had endured and witnessed in her life. As we pulled away, her pale face dissolved to an apparition. The streets receded. The onion domes glinted in the sunlight. Then they too were gone, obscured in dust as we drove on a dirt road that cut back to the highway. Behind us, lost in silence, stood the village of the forgotten.

Tomas held the steering wheel with one hand, and with the other rummaged in the glove box in search of a bottle opener. He handed it to me and pointed to the beer bottles on the back seat. I opened one and passed it over. He gulped it down and, when he was done, began humming the theme from *Love Story*.

We passed a caved-in farmhouse and, several kilometres further on, another. When neglected houses collapse, the chimney is the last to go. It remains long after the main structure is gone, like the teeth of long-decayed corpses. We passed a barn bulging with fodder. Strands poked through cracks and spilt through the open doorway. The landscape was familiar, yet alien.

Late morning we arrived at the outskirts of the Bialowieza Forest and, soon after, we veered off the highway onto an
overgrown track. Tomas stopped in a clearing. Armed with a
chainsaw, he disappeared and returned every ten minutes with
sawn logs and branches. He firmly refused my offers of help. This
was his domain, his purchase on pride and competence.

After one last foray, he brought back a hessian sack filled
with mushrooms and set about building a fire. Despite his size,
Tomas appeared at ease, unencumbered. The heavy boots and
the lumbering gait, which had appeared so ungainly the previous
day, now had about them a touch of lightness. As the fire died
down he placed a blackened pot over the embers. He cut the
stalks off as he waited for the water to boil, and then threw in the
mushrooms.

He worked methodically. When the mushrooms were done,
he served them with oil and vinegar on tin plates. He unwrapped
the sandwiches and placed them beside the mushrooms. We ate
in silence. Language was a barrier, except for the smattering of
German that Tomas had acquired as a guest worker. Besides, by
nature he was not talkative. It didn't matter. He had prepared
and served food with care and attention. His gesture spoke
volumes.

If only Stefan and Katrina could see him at his work, I
couldn't help thinking. If only they could appreciate his attention to detail, and his knowledge of the borderlands. And the
pride he took in being of service. Or perhaps they had seen it
often enough, and this too now repelled them.

I recalled Tomas as I had seen him the previous night,

curled up within himself like an infant, and my first sight of him, stooping beneath the lintel, reduced in stature despite his height and physical vigour, his helplessness in the presence of his wife and son, and the aching distance between them. In stark contrast, in the forest he was fully alive, fully present.

Mid-afternoon Tomas dropped me off at a lodge by the forest. He insisted on carrying my backpack into the foyer. I accompanied him back outside. He stood by the truck, unsteady on his feet, and grasped my right hand. He would not let go of it.

At some point in the previous hour, he had crossed a threshold. The balance between sobriety and inebriation had tilted. The ease and competence I had seen in the forest was gone. His bloodshot eyes veered between powerlessness and menace. They drew me in and held me. It was writ large in those bloody rivulets: the longing for communion, and the hint of a rage that could burst into fury. Or so I imagined.

In the hours we had driven on the road, we had barely exchanged a word. Yet I knew. I knew more than enough, and I felt for him. And I was relieved when he let go of my hand and climbed back into the cabin.

The sun was low, all but obscured by the foliage. I looked downwards as I walked, late afternoon, in the forest. Frogs hid in the undergrowth. Flies lay ensnared on spiderwebs, fallen oaks were entangled in greenery. The forest floor was moist, layered with leaves and pine needles, swarming with small life: fungi, mosses, herbs and mushrooms, vines snaking up massive trunks, living and dead matter embracing. All was still apart from a single bird call and the intermittent shriek of insects.

A sudden radiance of late afternoon sun flared in a clearing. Yet even here, as in many nearby places, there were markers of mass graves, sites of massacre, where Nazi battalions had hunted down and murdered partisans and civilians. I was struck by the irony: so much sun-dappled beauty, yet so much slaughter. There was no way out, nowhere to avoid it.

Years later I would come to know the numbers. Here in the borderlands between 1933 and 1945 some fourteen million unarmed people were murdered. They were starved, shot or gassed. Most were women and children, and the aged. These figures do not include the millions of armed soldiers killed in the same area in frontline combat.

'Bloodlands', the historian Timothy Snyder calls the area ranging from central Poland to western Russia, from the Black Sea to the Baltic, from the Ukraine through Belarus to Lithuania, Latvia and Estonia. And even here, in these last remains of primeval forest that once spread across the plains of Europe.

At this moment I stood at the geographical epicentre. Even though I did not know the figures then, I was overcome by the sheer magnitude of what had transpired here. So many deaths, so much wanton murder.

I returned to the lodge and lay back on the bed exhausted. Through my window I could make out conifers swaying. The exposed roof beams and the timber panelling were giving way to darkness. The events of recent days weighed heavily. The images of the months of travel and what I had come upon in the past hour were a confusing jumble: the tangled undergrowth, the markers of mass graves, the posies of flowers. The confusion amplified, somehow, by Tomas's bloodshot eyes, Stefan's pale complexion, Katrina's desperation. And a silver music box, like a wounded bird, playing a song of irretrievable love and shattered promises.

Capriccio

The road to Puchalski's cottage runs east through the border-lands, and Andrei is laughing, for the smooth curving of the asphalt beneath his Skoda, the midday sun that pierces the gaps in the passing forest, for the pure joy of it. An amber neck-lace glints against his black jumper. He drapes one arm around Halinka's shoulders and, with the other, he grips the steering wheel. Marek and I are in the back seat, Andrei's violin between us. Golden autumn, the Poles call it, season of mellow mists and fruitfulness as Keats would have it, though we will have to wait until nightfall for the mists.

Andrei is not a man who waits. There is something he wishes to show us. He skids the car to a stop. We follow him on the path that cuts into the forest. A scattering of cones lies on the pathway. An anthill teems with busy workers. We stop to pick blueberries as Andrei moves ahead to a pine tree.

'The pine is the violinist's tree,' he says. Andrei jabs his finger at the crimson resin bleeding from the trunk. 'It provides the rosin for the bow. It adds friction to the hair. Without rosin there is no sound when the bow is applied to the strings.'

Andrei takes off his necklace and points out the individual beads. Embedded within each bead are dark spots, spidery veins. 'They are insects, slivers of bark, fragments of leaves,' he says, 'ancient remnants trapped in the past like embalmed mummies.'

'Andrei! You are running ahead of yourself,' says Marek, a forest ranger and biologist. 'Before we can talk of amber and what lies trapped within it, we need to understand that the resins are toxic hydrocarbon secretions that protect the tree from herbivores. It takes millennia for them to harden into the fossilised resins that we call amber.'

'A few thousand years, give or take, what does it matter,' says Andrei. He is restless, anxious to be on the move. 'Amber traps the past, that is the point. It is a reflection of the Polish temperament,' he laughs.

'Like the amber, we too hold onto the past. Some nations look forward, others live in the moment, but our gaze is turned backward. We are trapped by what has taken place, burdened by the presence of the empires that flank us—Germany to the west, the Soviets to the east. We see ourselves as victims squeezed between predators, a nation of underdogs. I wear the amber necklace because it reminds me to live for the day, lest this be my maudlin fate.'

On our return to the Skoda Andrei wraps his arms round Halinka's waist. He runs his hands over her dress, gently pushes up the hem and brushes his fingers over her thighs. She leans into him and encircles her arms around his shoulders with the ease of a lover. They embrace on the verge in full view of the passing traffic.

Halinka is barely beyond her teens and Andrei is well into his forties. With his athlete's physique, unblemished blue eyes, tanned skin and blond hair tied back in a ponytail, he exudes the vigour of a twenty-year-old. 'I don't give a damn,' he shouts at the heavens. 'I don't give a damn.' He lifts Halinka into the air in a flight of exuberance, and sets her down with the deftness of a ballet dancer.

We resume our places and drive on. The forest yields to fields of oats and barley. Strands of flax lie drying on the earth, thistles wave on the roadside. We come upon an enclave of datchas, summer vacation houses barely larger than one-room cabins. The fenced gardens are luxuriant with vegetables and flowers, the houses defined by individual touches, unique designs and colours.

'That's how it is in Poland,' laughs Marek. 'This is what the old farts and collaborators who talk endlessly about building Communism have succeeded in creating. We know that despite their fine words the apparatchiks are lining their own pockets. The Party enables them to advance while they drone on about revolution. So we tend our tiny private plots, fence them in, protect them, and pour our energy into our little datchas. Small as they are, they mean more to us than any collective venture.'

'It is our one big "Fuck you" to those who want to control us,' laughs Andrei. Halinka lights a cigarette, leans over and places it between his lips. 'Jaruzelski, our current president, is the biggest fart of them all,' he says, 'a Soviet stooge. We have a joke that defines him.

'Jaruzelski craves the people's love, so he approaches God and says, "Please God, give me something that will gain me the people's respect." God takes pity on him and grants him the power to walk on water. Jaruzelski calls a public holiday in Warsaw. The people assemble on the banks of the Vistula, having been promised a display of powers that will astonish them. Bands are playing, stalls are selling food, children are running wild. The crowds are in a festive mood at this unexpected respite from their labours. At the appointed hour, to a fanfare of trumpets, Jaruzelski begins to walk on the water. He possesses miraculous powers. "Surely the people will admire me now," he thinks. But all along the banks the spectators are jabbing each other in the ribs, whispering, "Look at the poor bastard, he can't even swim."'

We return to our private thoughts. I am warming to this region of drowsy hamlets, lakes and forests. There are few remaining traces of my ancestors, but after two months of moving about I am coming to understand why poets have sung the praises of these borderlands, their vast tracts of untamed wildness.

Farmlands yield back to forest. Marek directs Andrei to stop and leads us along a path to a forest clearing. There are six mounds in the clearing, each thirty or so metres in length, twenty in width, and each dotted by white and mauve chrysanthemums, marigolds and the occasional posy of plastic flowers. There are up to one hundred bodies buried in each mound, proclaims a sign by the entrance to the clearing.

'My father was a Polish soldier. He was shot here in the autumn of 1939,' says Marek. 'I was ten at the time.' He speaks plainly, as one who has lived with this all his life. 'Years can go by between visits, but on each return I have the same thought. I work with trees every day. I know them better than I know people. Many of the trees that overlook the clearing are more than one hundred years old. They are the same trees my father would have seen before he closed his eyes for the last time.'

He bends down, places an oil lamp on one of the mounds and lights the wick. 'These borderlands are criss-crossed with mass graves. I am a scientist, but science cannot explain this cruelty. I cannot fathom it. How can people kill on such golden days, surrounded by so much radiance?'

We hear a tractor beyond the forest, approaching, receding, and the whir of a chainsaw. 'Let's get out of here or we'll end up singing sad songs,' laughs Andrei. 'At this rate we'll never make it to Puchalski's cottage. I did not come back to Poland to spend my time brooding over corpses.'

We drive on for an hour and stop for lunch in a hamlet by a river. The streets are ablaze with flowers. They grow by the road-sides, in cottage gardens and in pots and jars on windowsills. On the door of one cottage hangs a print of Van Gogh's *Sunflowers*, and in the front garden sunflowers nod under blue skies like live replicas. 'Welcome to my uncle's humble abode,' says Andrei with a mock flourish.

In the living room hangs a painting of a horse-drawn sleigh

pulling up in the snow outside a thatched cottage, and, on the opposite wall, a woven tapestry of a bowl of flowers. Like the Van Gogh on the door, the tapestry complements the vases of fresh flowers that sit on the mantelpiece and on top of the bookshelf. A cocker spaniel bounds up to our feet, panting with excitement.

Andrei's ageing uncle serves a vegetable broth with sour cream, followed by a main course of chicken schnitzel. The talk is of Solidarnosc, the clandestine movement opposing decades of dictatorial rule and Soviet occupation. On the bookshelf stands a framed photo of the movement's leader, Lech Walesa. In the autumn of 1986, the movement's appeal is palpable. The people are stirring. Growing in daring. Openly mocking their puppet leaders, buoyed by a sense of comradeship that arises in times of underground activity. Marek is hopeful of change.

But Andrei is sceptical. 'The counter insurgency police are everywhere,' he says. 'And they are determined to put down the revolt for one simple reason: their livelihoods depend on it. As do the livelihoods of the party apparatchiks and their hangers-on. They are not going to let go of their privileges without a dog-fight.'

Solidarnosc is of the present, but Andrei's uncle slips back into the past. In contrast to the wary optimism of the movement, he has an older way of thinking. His story is a variation on many I have heard in recent months. It is a story that Andrei does not wish to hear again. He lights a cigarette and steps outside as his uncle launches into the telling.

Andrei was born, he says, on the eve of war, in a town now located on the Soviet side of the border. The family retreated to

Warsaw, as the Germans crossed the Narew and Bug rivers and attacked the Soviet Union in 1941. He and his brother, Andrei's father, joined the AK, the underground Home Army, the armed wing of the Polish resistance. They worked as couriers, engaged in sabotage and fought in the 1944 Warsaw Uprising.

The Red Army stood by on the banks of the Vistula as the retreating Germans reduced Warsaw to rubble, building by building, block by block. They set the city alight and levelled entire neighbourhoods, and left a network of live mines as their calling cards. As for the Allies, says Andrei's uncle, why would they intervene when it also suited them to allow Poland to be fatally wounded?

When the German occupiers left, the Soviets entered what remained of Warsaw as triumphant liberators. The city smelt of rotting corpses. Here and there stood a lone chimney, a shattered fireplace. The streets were littered with disembowelled mattresses and hunchbacked street lamps. People clawed the debris in search of a family memento. Others gazed vacantly or sat in the ruins. One crazed man stumbled about calling out the names of the disappeared. His madness was reaffirmed at each discovery of human remains. Each one released a howl of anguish and the realisation that a loved one was not returning.

Andrei's father survived the uprising but was badly wounded. He lived for five years after the war, long enough to witness one occupation supplanted by another, the Nazis by the Soviet over-lords and their puppets.

Andrei steps back into the room, and cuts his uncle short. 'Spare us the morbid details,' he says. 'Every Pole has their hard luck story. I survived and I have not done too badly. Thanks to the party purges in 1968 and the failure of the student protests, I finally saw the light and escaped. At least I have that to thank the apparatchiks for. They destroyed any illusions I still had for a better future.

'They enabled me to leave Poland with a clear conscience. *Tabula rasa.* I left singing and was reborn in Paris. I was free to roam the continent, a member of a reputable orchestra, free to cross borders without interrogations in the company of my fellow musicians. Free even to return here, to Poland, safe in the knowledge that I can leave whenever I wish. What more needs to be said? I found a way out, an escape from the curse called history.'

Andrei serves cheesecake and strawberries, and refills our glasses. 'Without vodka one can understand nothing,' he says, lifting his glass. 'And what one understands when sober is not worth knowing.'

We drive on in silence. The fields are streaked with afternoon sunlight. The Skoda overtakes a horse-drawn cart piled high with turnips on a bridge spanning the Narew River. A fisherman poles a boat between reeds and waterlilies. Downstream, a horse walks aimlessly in a cemetery above the riverbank. The sun is well on the descent when we finally reach our destination.

Puchalski's log cottage is located in a hamlet. In the yard of a neighbouring cottage, a babushka hauls a pail of feed to a pigsty. Two storks perch on a thatched roof on a gigantic nest constructed around a cartwheel. 'There are few storks here now,' says Marek. 'Most are on their annual migrations.'

'Unlike our pathetic species, they do not require visas,' butts in Andrei.

Marek unlocks the door to the cottage. Rattan baskets and bunches of herbs hang from the ceiling beams. Neatly placed about the room are wooden mortars and pestles, fish traps, a weaving loom and reed sandals designed for wading through marshland. There are woodcarvings of bison and deer, elk and eagles. Crucifixes dangle beside strings of corn and garlic. Cooking utensils hang from wall hooks. Two wooden ducks, once used as floating lures for male geese in the swamplands, sit on the mantelpiece.

'Welcome to the home of Wlodzimierz Puchalski,' says Marek, 'photographer, filmmaker, Antarctic explorer, forest ranger, lover of wildlife and wilderness. My friend and confidant, who, to my lasting regret, passed away seven years ago.'

His life was cut short by a heart attack, Marek tells us. He died while filming sea birds in the Antarctic. The cottage is preserved and cared for by friends and former colleagues. The contents are, more or less, as they were when he was last here. 'Puchalski coined the phrase "the bloodless hunt",' says Marek. 'Instead of tracking and killing wildlife, he stalked it with lenses and cameras.'

On the wall are photos of animals he had caught in situ, mid-movement. Two chicks crouch in a nest, beaks raised and wide open, about to be fed by the unseen mother. A bear lopes across a swampy paddock. Flocks of birds are snapped at the moment of rising. A squirrel perches precariously on a fungus extending horizontally from a tree trunk. On the table is a book of Puchalski's photos.

I flip through the pages. Frogs face the camera poised for take-off. Rodents peer from hollows and burrows. Herds of elk and bison stampede down hillsides. Animal footprints disappear over a desolate snowfield. Wild flowers bloom on mountain slopes. *Trofea Obiektywu*, Trophies of the Lens, the book is titled. Puchalski is pictured, surrounded by wetlands, binoculars hanging from his neck, tripod resting on his shoulders.

Above one doorway there are three owls made from pine branches, with acorns for eyes and pinecones for noses. 'The owls were carved by Puchalski's wife,' says Marek, 'to represent the three members of the immediate family: mother, father and daughter. Their happiest times were spent here in the cabin.'

Marek directs us to an oak trunk opposite the fireplace. It is full of books and papers. A letter is glued inside the lid. Dated August 22 1971, it is addressed to the house and signed by Puchalski: 'Farewell my house, my treasured haven of silence and rest, source of happiness and beautiful moments spent under the shade of the roof. I would like to sit here for a while. Be for the guests what you always used to be for me. Farewell.'

'When he wrote these words, perhaps he felt he didn't have long to live,' says Marek. We sit by the oak table and toast Puchalski with vodka. The farewell note has made us welcome. Thrown together by chance days earlier, in this moment we share a sense of camaraderie. With each passing minute our faces recede further into darkness. Outside the birch and oak trees rustle. The stone woodstove waits for the return of the fire; the cottage is a still life, poised for the imminent return of its owner.

We would gladly sit here for hours but Andrei, who has not spoken since we entered, is restless. His bravado has evaporated, as has his youthful exuberance. Within this cottage there is no veil of pretence, no cover for his bitterness. The tranquillity has unnerved and unmasked him.

Halinka places a hand on his hands, which are resting on the table. Against Andrei's hers are like the tiny chicks in one of Puchalski's photos, dwarfed by the nest that protects them. 'Compared to humans, the wildlife that Puchalski stalked with his cameras are saints,' says Andrei, breaking the silence. His voice floats towards us as if from a distance.

'There are things that can never be understood,' he says, 'that words cannot do justice. Everyone around here knows what happened, even those who deny it. It is all about us, like a cancer. The symptom that gives us away is our constant weariness. We are tired, my friend,' he says, addressing me, the passing traveller.

'We know how much blood has flowed in these border-lands, and the endless battles that have been waged here. We know that one generation ago, people hid out there,' he says, pointing his thumb over his shoulder, 'within walking distance, in the swamps and marshes, among the reeds and thickets that grow on the banks of the Narew, those beautiful places Puchalski loved to photograph. They were hunted down—men, women and children—and slaughtered.

'We were all caught in the madness. Words cannot convey what I witnessed as a child during the Warsaw Uprising: the shit that comes from fear, from being cornered in crumbling tenements and dead-end alleys; the stench of the sewers and cellars in which the fighters hid between street battles. They cannot do justice to the nobility of my father and uncle, the shadow world of the underground, and the Soviets' betrayal of our people, their act of abandonment.

'Words cannot convey my impotence in 1968, when my stepbrother fell to his death. He was pushed from a building in the Warsaw University during the student protests. He naively believed that the regime would not turn on its own children. I cannot fathom the brutality of the thugs and stooges that are always ready to do the dirty work, the devil's bidding.'

Andrei's words have become a torrent, made all the more disturbing by the robotic tone of his telling and the grim smile we can see now that our eyes have adjusted to the darkness.

'During the Warsaw Uprising, my good friend, at the age of twelve, played dead. He extricated himself from a pile of corpses only to come back to life in a Poland that had fallen under the dead weight of yet another dictatorship. He now lives in Brussels and works as a journalist; he stuffs himself with drink and trivial information, and is lost in a lust for women that can never be sated.'

Andrei's tirade unnerves us. The cottage has grown smaller. Its thick oak door and log walls no longer feel solid; they seem like the timber shell of a penetrable fortress. 'Words conceal more than they reveal,' he adds after a silence. 'They cannot convey how I longed to get away, yet how, within days of leaving, I long to return—the curse of nostalgia. They cannot convey the lure of the fields and forests of my childhood, the paradox that is the history of my country.'

Andrei pauses. 'I cannot bear the sound of my own voice,' he resumes. 'I wish to take back all I have said. Someone else is in control, a pious ventriloquist. What do I know or care about politics? The one language I trust is of musical notes and the silences between them.'

When we leave, Marek locks the door behind us. The evening has descended and the wind is rising. 'This is a perfect time for a performance,' says Andrei. 'Before we drive home, a salute to Puchalski.' He takes out his violin from the Skoda. He puts the case down on the ground, lifts out the bow, and runs it across the rosin. Showers of powder spit from the bow like fireflies. Once done, he raises the violin to his shoulder.

'Paganini was the violinist of violinists,' he says. 'He wanted to attain the impossible. His hands were so big they enabled him to do what many other violinists could not. But still it was not enough, it is never enough. No matter how hard the artist tries, no matter what skill he brings to the task, he can never replicate the terror and beauty we call living.

'But the artist tries. Paganini tried. He was obsessed with composing music that stretched his skills beyond the limits. He was an egotistical bastard, like me, but he lived without pretence and allowed his appetites to take him. He was mad, and his madness can be heard in his music. He poured his lust and longing into his work, and that is why I love him, and why I love to play him. Besides, my large hands are well suited to his compositions.'

Andrei tunes the violin, and readies himself for playing. 'I salute you my dear pine,' he says with mock irony, turning his face towards the copses of birch and conifers on the outskirts of the hamlet. 'For you I play Paganini. It is my gift to the forest in exchange for the amber and the rosin.'

He plays a Paganini capriccio. The notes rise sharply and tear apart the silence. Birds, startled from their evening roosts, break clear of the woodlands. Hares scatter as if pursued by a predator. A horse whinnies and takes off to the far end of a paddock. The two storks rise from their giant nest and vanish into the heavens.

Capriccio, in its original seventeenth-century French and Italian, means 'a shivering'. The word is said to have derived from *capro* 'goat', a frisking goat, or from *capo* meaning 'head', plus *riccio* 'curled and frizzled'. Hence, as one dictionary puts it, 'a person, shivering in fear', and 'a head with the hair standing on end'. From there, it is just a small step to 'a sense of horror'. Over time capriccio has come to mean a sudden start, and when applied to human behaviour, a whim, an unaccountable turn of mind. An act of impulse.

Andrei plays with a controlled fury. Out in the open we can discern the nuances: the artistry that extends beyond Paganini's frenzied compositions, the variations in pace, and phrases in which each note can be heard with utter clarity. He moves effortlessly from bow to pizzicato, and returns to the bow for the crescendo. Beyond this small circle of friends extend the mysteries of the night, the dim outlines of trees and their shadows.

The final notes give way to a moment of stillness. Then the landscape formulates a reply that will outlive the music: a single bird call, the rustle and scurry of small things and, further afield, more imagined than heard, the hum of the marshes. And, suddenly, a chorus of frogs croaking in the swamplands.

The birds are taking up the roosts they had abruptly forsaken. The storks too are returning. Despite their size they land noiselessly on the thatched roof, legs extended forward and, moments later, they perch on their massive nests, motionless. All is being restored to order. The onslaught is over.

The Wall

Nina Simone, the descendant of slaves in North Carolina, is singing 'Pirate Jenny', a song about an enraged servant girl, written for an opera set in nineteenth-century London, and first performed in Berlin, in 1928. And I am listening to the song playing on a turntable in a wine bar in West Berlin, on an October night in 1986, on a day that had begun at dawn in Warsaw, as the Berlin express left the central station.

The train had broken free from the underground tube into the city fringes, hurtling past apartment buildings where crows perch on chimneys and TV antennae, and into the countryside past fields with bales of hay and ploughed furrows, past clusters of birch and forests of conifers, the morning frosts lifting—images I had seen over the previous three months of travel across the length of the Soviet Empire from Beijing to Moscow, and via Warsaw back to the borderlands of eastern Poland.

The train had slowed at the East German frontier to that strained silence that ensues before the boarding of frontier police, the stillness broken by dogs snarling, the bark of voices and the crunch of boots on gravel. And within seconds the carriage was swarming with uniformed men in jackboots, three in my compartment: one sullen, a second inflated with anger, the third smiling like a contented lover.

One of them stood over me, scrutinising my passport. He was sizing me up, his eyes moving between my face and the photo, while his colleagues poked torches beneath the seats and overhead at the luggage racks. The officer continued his inspection, directing me to open my backpack, rifling through my belongings, scattering my possessions over the seat as if upending a bag of rubbish.

Then, as abruptly as it had begun, it was over. The police were gone, our passports stamped, transit visas granted, leaving us to pass through a country that had become a vast prison, and a mystery—the passengers insulated within the fast-moving train from the passing landscape and its people.

But the carriages could not entirely shield us from glimpses of everyday incidents, mundane rituals: elderly men and women sunning themselves on wooden benches; a solitary woman tending a village graveyard; two men seated at a card table on a station platform, deep in concentration over a game of chess; school children walking hand in hand on a village pathway; a man riding a bicycle on a country road, head bent low against the wind under an avenue of poplars.

Mid-afternoon I caught my first sight of the Berlin Wall from a carriage window. From this distance, and from the height of the railway embankment, the wall appeared smaller than I had anticipated. My expectations had been inflated by the mystique that had enveloped the wall during the quarter of a century since workers began laying the barbed wire barriers that would seal off West Berlin from escaping East German citizens.

At the West Berlin station there were no border troops or customs officials. No one was remotely interested in my documents. I stepped from the station into the city with a heady lightness, as if let loose after months of confinement.

West Berlin on first impression, in sharp contrast to the city I had left that morning, was an assault of competing choices, brazen and anarchic. Naked women winked from billboards; shop windows blazed with designer-label fashions. Music blared from shopping emporiums. Neon signs blinked the colour spectrum. This is a city, I had heard said, that knows how to party.

I continued walking as the evening chill descended, finding my way, disoriented, to the wine bar, where I listen to the strident voice of Nina Simone, recorded in live performance. Her singing is savage and urgent. She has bent Bertolt Brecht's libretto to her own image. She is Pirate Jenny as a black servant girl, down on her knees in a rundown hotel, in a racist southern town, scrubbing the floor, while her masters are smirking and gawking. Her voice is an accusation, her singing an act of defiance.

The song takes hold of me and accompanies my hours of walking, my inspection of the wall with its scrawls and inscriptions, artworks and graffiti, its brooding presence. Since the divide was established, the barbed wire had been fortified with electric fences and reinforced concrete, and an inner fence marking off a stretch of no-man's-land. Up to one hundred metres in width, this stretch had become known as the 'death strip'.

I seek out vantage points from which to see the faces of the armed guards who stand, guns at the ready, in watchtowers. The sun reflects off their binoculars. The drab buildings beyond them are wrapped in mystery. The sentry boxes look out over the wall into the death strip, a sharp reminder of the dire consequences of escaping.

Yet many had tried: jumping from apartment windows, digging tunnels from cellars and graveyards, building cars low enough to drive beneath the traffic barriers, crashing trucks through the gates and fences. Smuggling themselves out in car boots and hidden compartments. Firing arrows from a rooftop attached to a nylon cord, swinging over on pulleys. Stitching a hot-air balloon from scraps of curtains and bedding, flying ultra-lights. And many had been killed or maimed fleeing for their lives through a barrage of searchlights and bullets, over anti-vehicle trenches and barbed wire barriers.

It is four decades since the Second World War ended, and twenty-five years since the wall was erected, and yet the conflict is not over. World war had been supplanted by cold war, countries split apart, families divided. And there is talk of odd things happening in the death strip, of rodents and wild rabbits that have colonised this narrow stretch of wasteland, and are feeding on its wild grasses. But their sojourn may soon be ended. There are whispers of a day of reckoning, when the wall will be torn apart and the concrete hacked to rubble. Talk of dictators being sent packing, the apparatus of surveillance disassembled, and of old scores being exposed and settled.

And all the while Nina Simone is singing of vengeance. She is a servant girl gritting her teeth and grinning, biding her time, dreaming of the black freighter with the skull and crossbones on its masthead making its way into the harbour. She is waiting for the coming of her redeemers. Her deliverance.

Her voice accompanies me at dawn several days later as I walk from my hotel room towards the station. It is raining and a cold wind is howling. I am haunted by the wall, its solidity, and the contrast between the two sides: one blank and devoid of colour, the other layered with caricatures of dictators, slogans and profanities, tags and scribbles, declarations of love, mini treatises on freedom. Haunted too by infamous images of the wall when under construction, slicing the heart of the city, cutting off brother from sister, child from parent, fracturing families who stood in clusters, waving to each other across the divide, clutching kerchiefs, weeping.

I hear the song's rhythms in the movement of the train, which is taking me back into East Germany. Border troops patrol the corridors. Vast tracts of woodland are alight with autumn reds and auburns. Vines cascade down mountainsides as we approach yet another no-man's-land: a strip of earth that cuts through a forest. We pass one last strand of barbed wire, a final surveillance post, and the train is through the last passport inspection point into West Germany.

At the first station after the border a woman walks along the platform handing out paper cups of tea to those who lean out of the windows. The train moves through the Bavarian country-side, past mediaeval towns and hamlets surrounded by field and forest. The landscape is well ordered, symmetrical, the land green and fertile. And within the hour I am walking through the streets of Nuremburg, address in hand, to an apartment on the edge of the inner city.

Anna is expecting me, but I have barely had time to set down my bags when she is urging me out, walking with me to a univer-sity cinema, to a showing of Murneau's 1920s black-and-white classic, *Faustus*, the tale of an elderly necromancer and alchemist, and his infamous pact with the devil. The film is shot in light and shadow, alternately illuminating and concealing facades and faces, accentuating the battle between good and evil, salvation and temptation. The student audience groans when the final word, *liebe*, appears on the screen, signalling the triumph of love. It is all too easy, they say, too simple.

'Welcome to Nuremburg,' says Anna on the way back to her apartment. She is aware of the lingering effect of the film, its bleak images, and the apt initiation that *Faustus* has provided for my brief stay in the city. She had planned it.

We had met months ago in the first weeks of my journey, as fellow travellers on an overnight train heading from southern China to Beijing. Even then, in our few hours of conversation, on hard seats in a crowded third-class compartment, I had observed her restlessness and learned of her obsession with her father and his former comrades and drinking companions.

'He was so kind to me when I was young,' she says, as if taking up a conversation that had been temporarily interrupted, disembarking at the Beijing station. A woman in her late twenties, Anna's English is correct, if somewhat formal. 'He was such a sweet and doting father, but when I was thirteen he began to control me. He accused me of being a cheap flirt and tried to prevent me from seeing my boyfriend. He watched my movements as if he were my keeper.

'He would come in at night, sit on my bed and ramble on for hours about his former girlfriends, trying to impress me, to ingratiate himself. "I am so tired," he would say. "Everything I do is for you," he claimed. He was such a weary, beaten man, with the eyes of a cornered animal.

'I just wanted him to go away, to let me be. I began to suspect that he harboured a secret, a sinister past he shared with his drinking companions. I ran away from the town I was raised in as if from the devil, and came to Nuremberg. I fell in love with the city, and the freedom it offered me.

'It was a crazy, wonderful time. I studied nursing, had my share of lovers, and came to know these streets and the city's Renaissance history. Nuremberg was a centre for craftsmen and artists, free thinkers and progressives, a city of the Reformation. I fell in love with Albrecht Dürer, with his woodcut prints and engravings, his altarpieces. Such intricate beauty. Such precision. You must see his work. Tomorrow we will visit his house and workshop.'

Anna pauses. The animation drains from her face like a

photo returning to its negative. I do not know what has brought it about, but in the ensuing days I will come to see the pattern of her oscillations—the freedom in her movement, and an air of worldliness acquired from years of travel and introspection, succumbing, without notice, to bouts of doubt and obsession.

'Just when I thought I had secured my independence,' she says, 'my father came to fetch me. He forced me into his car and threatened to beat me. He drove wildly through the city. His body was trembling with anger. It was to be the last time. I searched the passing streets for an opening. This was my advantage. The city was my ally. For the first time in my father's presence I was calm and calculating.

'At a red light I opened the door and jumped out and disappeared into the alleys I knew so well, and as I ran, I was laughing. Everything seemed comical: the gothic buildings, the sight of my shoes hurrying over the cobblestones, and the earnest, hard-working citizens hurrying by. I couldn't stop laughing.

'Nuremburg is beautiful, don't you think?' she says, her spirits lifting. We do not want to let go of the night. The pavements are dimly lit by streetlamps. Buildings follow the natural contours of the river. Flowers spill from window boxes. Cathedral spires pierce the heavens. Flights of steps spiral up to the ramparts of a castle.

The city was reconstructed from the ruins left after the allied air raids, Anna tells me. The carpet-bombing had reduced Nuremberg to debris. The mediaeval centre was destroyed. Thousands of citizens were killed or displaced. The survivors reconstructed the cobbled streets and landmark buildings, stone by stone, brick by brick. Within a decade almost all had been restored to its pre-war grandeur. All is correct, all is in order.

Yet Pirate Jenny is seething. She is on her knees, scrubbing and cleaning. Silently scheming. And the gentlemen are barking: *Hey gal, finish them floors! Get upstairs! What's wrong with you? Earn your keep here!* They are tossing their tips, proud of their largesse, condescending. They cannot see that the servant girl is furtively glancing at the harbour. She is looking out for the black freighter, biding her time, planning her day of reckoning.

And Anna, too, is not done yet. The ghosts are returning. She reminds me that Nuremberg was the spiritual centre of Nazism, the backdrop to Hitler's imperial aspirations, his dreams of a Reich that would impose its rule for a millennium.

'If you want to meet the former Nazis,' she says, 'I can show you the pubs where they drink and play cards. Harmless men like my uncle, turning old and senile.' Again the vibrancy is draining from her face. Her speech slows. The tone has flattened. She speaks as if she is elsewhere.

'You know, my grandmother helped a Jewish friend escape before the war. She was photographed and her photo was published in one of the party's rags with the caption, 'Jew lover'. My uncle, her son-in-law, and fourteen years her junior, came to the house whip in hand and flogged her.

'I don't know exactly how old I was when I heard this story, but it deeply distressed me. I could no longer feel proud of who I was, of my family, my country. There were so many secrets. I did not want to think ill of my uncle. I did not want to see him as someone capable of such horror. As a child I loved him. I loved to play with him. He brought me sweets and presents. He was kind and gentle. He was good with children. And he was a Nazi.'

The following morning we take a train three kilometres south-east to the edge of the city, the site of the infamous rallies. We are dwarfed by our surroundings—the vast assembly areas, the Zeppelin field, the Great Road, and the grounds of the former Hitler Youth stadium—confronted by the circular Congress Hall, built in the image of the Roman Colosseum. It stands before our eyes, solid yet crumbling, built to last, now decaying.

We approach the tiered Tribune. One hundred and fifty metres long, in its days of glory it was flanked by gold eagles, the cobblestone terrace lined with two rows of torch pillars. Fourteen pylons remain standing, decomposing. The sheer scale of the rally grounds and its structures overwhelms us.

The site conjures the menacing spectacle of the masses that first assembled here in 1927 and continued assembling annually over the ensuing decade: devotees of a blood cult marching in torchlight processions, black shirts and brown shirts bearing a flag said to be soaked in the blood of one of the Beer Hall Putsch rebels. And marching with them, steel-helmeted soldiers and entranced civilians, armies of the night arrayed in perfect symmetry—arms outstretched in robotic unison, paying homage to the Fuehrer.

The ritual marked an era of genocide and horror, and among its victims were my four grandparents, two shot, two gassed, along with many of their children, and their extended families. An entire community. I look again, and see the site as it is on this cool autumn day, an ageing edifice to delusions of grandeur.

Anna is visibly anguished. 'There are times I want to run to the ends of the earth,' she says, 'and be rid of the sweet old men who so easily committed murder. I see their eyes and hands crawling over my skin, invading my being. They pursue me in my dreams, begging me to return to the fold. In one instant they are kind, in the next, grotesque. They are my own flesh and blood and I want to forgive them. But I think of the deeds they must have committed, and I cannot. I dream of my father and uncle, one on each arm: my captors.

'My father now says he would do anything for me, that he is proud of my achievements. "Do you have enough money?" he asks. "Do you have enough to eat? Can I get you a drink?" He comes to me contrite and pathetic, with flowers, and tempts me to feel sorry for him. He wants me to love him, to turn back the clock and be his little daughter.

'My uncle and father—their sickly sweet presence, their secrets—this is why I am always running, getting out, but always returning. There are times, when I am far away, that I am sure I have finally outrun their shadow. But no matter how far and how long I travel, I find myself back in Nuremberg, the city where I first sensed freedom.

'Then, within months, it palls again. I cannot get rid of my confusion: Nuremberg, of the rallies, Nuremberg, the place of my liberation. I know all too well where the ageing comrades meet with my father and uncle. I dream of bursting into their places where they sit over their beers and secrets, and tear to shreds their silences. I want them to tell me straight what they did, and be done with it. I have imagined the scene many times, my day of reckoning, but I know I can't do it. Instead I flee.'

Anna's torment verges on rage, and Pirate Jenny is counting the heads even as she's making the beds, because she knows that nobody's going to sleep here tonight, nobody. And there's a scream in the night and you see her staring out the window. The ship, the black freighter is turning in the harbour, and Jenny is rejoicing, because the guns will wipe the smile off the gentlemen's faces, and this whole damn place is going to be burnt to the ground. Only this cheap hotel will remain safe and sound.

Nina Simone's 'Pirate Jenny' brings to mind other songs, taught by my elders, performed throughout my childhood: *It's burning, brothers, it's burning, our impoverished shtetl is burning.* Songs of the feats of children who stole through the sewers, and smuggled in bottles and fuel that were fashioned into Molotov cocktails and broken-down pistols that locksmiths restored and readied for battle. Lullabies sung by mothers to provide a moment of comfort within the terror: *Close your eyes my dear one, birds are coming; they assemble here my child, by the pillow on your bed.* Songs they clung to on their final journeys. Songs of quiet despair and defiance, *Quiet, quiet, hush be silent, corpses are growing here.* Songs of partisan poets who drew upon the yearning of their people, and songs of hope and vengeance, sung in underground schools, at clandestine gatherings and in the heat of camp uprisings. Of ghetto fighters leaping from buildings, bursting through flames and scorched debris, and of partisans wading through swamps and assembling in forest hideouts on the eve of battle.

And I recall the first time I heard Nina perform the song, in New York, circa 1970, stalking the stage in Central Park in front of an audience of thousands. Then sitting down at a grand piano, pounding the keys, and grabbing the mic to resume her stalking. She is enraged, refusing to sing, haranguing the audience, berating and cajoling.

It is years since the event, yet I recall the essence of what she was saying. She rails against the recent jailing of black activists, and at the death of black children in church bombings, at the assassinations and lynching. She recounts the tale of her debut as a classical pianist, at the age of eleven, in North Carolina, when her parents were asked to move from the front to the back row just as their daughter was about to begin her first public performance. And in an act of rebellion, she had refused to play until they were allowed back to their seats in the front row. 'This is how it is,' she says. 'This is how it's been for too long now. Can't you see it? If you don't like what I'm saying, get out. I'm not going to sing for you, goddamn it.'

The crowd is thinning; the disgruntled concertgoers are leaving. The rain has set in as a gentle drizzle. And Nina turns to the audience. Her rage has drained. Her voice has softened. 'Y'all are so beautiful,' she says. 'Y'all stayed with me despite the rain. You've weathered the storm. It's a pleasure to sing for you.'

She performs for hours, a lithe, regal black woman, alternating between the stage floor and the piano: songs of sinner-men and angels in the morning, of would-be messiahs sinking like stones in the water, of black bodies swaying in the southern breeze, of children sitting in jail and lovers parting, of willows that are no longer weeping, and of chilled winds that are no longer blowing. And of Pirate Jenny, who is boarding the ship, the black freighter, and sailing out of the harbour now that her slave-masters have been vanquished.

High-rise apartment buildings wrap the park. They are barely visible through a veil of showers, and as Nina sings the metropolis is disappearing. All that exists is the voice of a performer for whom singing is an exorcism, a matter of survival, and perhaps a way to stave off an encroaching madness. She sings until it is midnight by the clock, and justice has been done, and the black freighter is vanishing out to sea. The struggle is finally over, and the crowds are dispersing, making their way home, invigorated by the ferocity of her performance.

The afternoon sun lights the Nuremburg Tribune. Learner drivers are cruising the weed-infested runway. Nearby, circus performers are unloading their gear, erecting tents, feeding lions and elephants. Autumn leaves are being swept into piles by city gardeners, and a family is setting out a picnic in the parklands.

I turn to Anna and embrace her. We are brother and sister, daughter and son of perpetrator and survivor, of the damned and the haunted: the offspring of history's madness. Releasing each other from its elusive shadow.

Threnody

There was a time when language and song were one, when to speak was to sing, and when the song was a cry of rage against an unforgiving sea, an impassive sky. And this is how it was, eight years ago on the island of Ithaca, with the death of a boy.

The boy's father was born and raised in the Village of the Forty Saints. He grew up surrounded by sea and, like many young men of the island, he was schooled in the maritime arts. For ten years he worked as a seaman on cargo boats. He berthed on every continent, and sailed from Gdansk to Napoli, from the Baltic to the Mediterranean and to Southern Hemisphere ports.

In time the allure of foreign lands began to pall. On each return to the island he found it harder to depart. He no longer felt the thrill of the first approach of land, that surge of anticipation as the ship moved towards a new port. He longed to stay put.

When he retired from seafaring he found work as the secretary of the villages on the northern heights. He issued licences and permits, and collected information on births, marriages and deaths. He presided over disputes concerning title deeds and took note of complaints. But the sea remained his grand passion, his first love.

He acquired a fishing caique and had it moored in the port of Frikes, a twenty-minute ride by motorbike from his two-storey home above Afales Bay. He set off when the weather allowed. It could be dusk, or midnight or three in the morning when he set out, and dawn when he returned.

He would sail out beyond the breakwater and head north, shadowing the mountain range on the east coast. He rounded the northernmost cape to Afales Bay, where he would drop anchor and lay his nets. From the boat he could make out his home above the cliffs and the clusters of lights that marked the villages on the upper slopes. He ventured further and came to know the fishing grounds off neighbouring isles.

When his son was born he was overjoyed. He took him out to sea before he was able to walk. The boy came to know the movements and habits of particular fish, and the caves and crevices where they lurked. He came to know the coves on nearby islands where they would shelter from sudden storms.

He came to know what lay beneath the waters. Father and son donned snorkels and masks and dived deep, spear guns in hand. They snared their share of fish, but dived also for the pleasure of identifying rare species. They took photos of seabeds littered with refuse cast from passing ferries and freighters. They wrote stories on Ionian sea lore and pollution, and had them published in journals of marine life.

Father and son would be seen on the motorbike, the boy clinging to his father, careering down from the village on the descent to the port and skidding to a halt by the breakwater where the boat was permanently moored.

The boy graduated from high school and enrolled in university to study mathematics. He stayed with relatives in Athens during the semesters but whenever time allowed he returned home. His life was a cyclical movement from island to mainland, from village to Athens, and the homecoming to Ithacan ports, his father waiting by the quay, then father and son on the familiar ascent by motorbike to the two-storey house overlooking Afales Bay.

He began his second year of study in the autumn of 2003. There was unrest brewing at the university. Lecturers and staff went out on strike. The campus was shut down, and the boy took advantage of this unexpected break.

It is a four-hour journey by ferry to Ithaca over the Ionian Sea from the port of Patras. The boy was always elated at the first sight of the island. It grew larger, seeming to rise as one land mass before separating into two islands as the ferry drew closer: the smaller island, Ithaca, in the foreground, and the mountain peaks of Kefalonia towering behind it.

The following morning the boy set out for a day of fishing.

He went down with his diving partner to the harbour beneath the village of Stavros. They call it 'the little summer of St Dimitri', this sojourn of sunny days before the onset of winter. It was the time of the olive harvest and the pickers were out in the groves.

The boys set sail from Polis Bay. They turned south and stayed close to the island on the west coast. They let down the anchor by an outcrop of rocks, adjusted their masks and snorkels, and eased themselves from the deck carrying spear guns. Just one hundred metres separated the boat from the limestone cliffs above the shore. The day was drifting towards the hour of siesta. Shopkeepers were drawing in their shutters, closing their doors. The school bus was wending its way back on the cliff road. The partners dived twice and surfaced. Then the boy decided on one more dive. When he did not surface his partner raised the alarm.

A wave of panic washed across the island. Fishing boats that had returned with their catches at dawn set sail in search of the boy. Islanders rushed to the waterfront, or picked their way down overgrown paths within sight of the outcrop of rocks.

His father knew that the boy was gone. 'He is no more,' he said. He shook his head and refused to be comforted by words of hope. Late afternoon, divers on a passing yacht retrieved the body. Church bells tolled the death for hours in an incessant monotone.

The boy was buried days later in the graveyard, overlooking the bays he had so often sailed. The church overflowed with the many islanders who had known him. Those who could not squeeze inside gathered on the terrace beneath the belltower.

Half the island was in attendance. The boy was loved for his good nature and generous spirit.

'He was more than a son,' said his father to the crowd. 'I have lost my companion, my best friend. There are no words that can describe my loss.'

We arrived on the island ten days after the boy, our nephew, drowned. We had known him since he was an infant. What we had planned as a family reunion was now a wake. At night we walked the streets of the village to the house overlooking Afales Bay. Every night Ithacans would come to the house to provide company. As is the custom, they would not allow the family to be alone in their grief.

We knew the familiar markers on the way from previous journeys: the satellite dishes rising from a neighbour's home, two white saucers hovering in the darkness like spacecraft; the bends in the road; and the sea vistas that open out at each turn. We walked past the crumbling shells of homes long abandoned and houses that had been restored by Ithacans returning after years abroad.

At night the northern heights are given over to wind gusts and barking dogs. The summer is long over and the season of hibernation is approaching. There are fewer lights with each passing week as houses close down for the winter. On clear nights, the villages in the neighbouring islands are scatterings of lights in swathes of dark. There are nights when the rains descend and lightning unveils the chapel on the heights, the jagged peaks and limestone ridges. Torrents pour upon the wooded slopes, yet still we make our way to the house.

We dread the first moments, the first sight of the stricken eyes of the boy's mother, her ongoing battle to comprehend what had taken place. We dread the depths of her disbelief at the calamity that has befallen her, and the dead weight upon her face. We dread the inconsolable anguish of the boy's grandmother.

The boy was her first grandchild and his death is an unbearable blow. She had looked after him since the day of his birth. She had comforted him through illnesses and rejoiced at his milestones and triumphs. Now she sits on a sofa in the lounge room and shakes her head. Grief is engraved on her face. It can never be erased. She clasps her hands in her lap and lifts them in a wringing gesture.

The straight back she had retained well into her ageing now sags in defeat. For the first time in the years that we have known her she is not attending her duties. She looks at us in bewilderment and falls into our arms like a wounded child. She is broken.

'*Ti na kanoume, ti na kanoume*,' she says. 'What can we do, what can we do?' She lapses back into silence. '*Ola ine tikhe, ola ine tikhe,*' she whispers. 'All is luck, all is fate.'

We hear the same refrain wherever we go. *Ti na kanoume*, the villagers say when the death of the boy is raised. *Ti na kanoume*, the goatherd says when we come across him driving his flock to mountain pastures. *Ti na kanoume*, says the physics professor as he ascends to the house he has built for his retirement. *Ti na kanoume*, the old seamen say as they bend over their cards in the coffee house.

They have endured their time at sea and long absences in distant lands. Now they sit by tables and wait for the end. Their cards fall onto the green felt hour upon hour. They are there every morning, return after the siesta, and remain long into the night. There is little that can affect them now. But they are deeply disturbed by the death of the boy. 'He left for the sea and never returned,' they say, and turn back to their cards.

'*Ti na kanoume,*' says a neighbour. 'The whole island is crying for him.' She adds her version of events: he was tired and weighed down by the fish tied to his waistband. He did not have a balloon attached by a line to his foot to indicate where he had gone down. His partner knew it was time to return to the boat after two dives, but he had insisted on one more. He was fearless, as the young so often are.

'There was something so beautiful about him this final summer,' she says, her eyes lost to the memory. 'He possessed the glow of youth.' She is trying to fathom the mystery, the unfairness that one so young should encounter such a fate. She shrugs, then sings:

> *Life has two doors*
> *I opened one,*
> *And came in one morning*
> *And by the time evening arrived*
> *I had left by the other*

She has always been tough, and tougher still in the past ten years since the untimely death of her husband. She opens the shutters every morning with a cigarette between her lips, waters her plants, and sets out for the olive groves with a chainsaw. Her body is strong and youthful for a woman of seventy. She has endured many seasons of labour and become hardened and stoic, but she cannot abide the death of the boy. 'He was so beautiful this last summer,' she whispers.

'*Ti na kanoume*,' says the boy's father when we see him next. It is near midnight. The house is full of smoke and talk, the gathering swelled by the continual arrival of family and friends. The boy's mother moves about like an apparition. With her helpers she has laid the table, poured the wine and served the fish and meat.

This is how it is night after night. Out of tragedy, a coming together. The mood has lifted as it does every night by this hour. There is banter and animated conversation. The talk is of politics and sport, the upcoming soccer match with the neighbouring island, analyses of recent matches, and the travails of the national team.

The boy's father and I step out. We walk from the house the short distance to the path beside the cliff. We see the familiar outline of the windmill. The sails are long gone, but the circular walls are intact. At this hour it is a dark presence on the crest of the mountain, at the point where the cliff road vanishes, several kilometres ahead.

We stop and look out over Afales Bay. I have stood here many times. It is my most treasured place on earth. Over the strait to the north can be seen a scattering of lights on the island of Lefkada. Just beyond are the white cliffs known as Sappho's Leap, where the poet of Lesbos is said to have thrown herself into the sea, propelled by unrequited love. So the story goes. Mountains rise behind us like tiers in a massive amphitheatre: the northern bays provide the stage, and the sea, the ongoing drama.

Directly behind us, lined up against a white stonewall, are sacks of olives, the spoils of one family's day in the groves. The sacks will be thrown onto the back of a utility and taken at dawn to the olive presses. On the darkened slopes are the family olive trees we have picked during previous stays. Below us the waves are washing up against a strip of pebbled beach at the cliff base. At all hours through the night, ferries make their way past en route to far-flung harbours.

'I was born overlooking the bay,' says the boy's father. 'I know every rock, every species of fish. I know where the fish will congregate when a particular wind blows. I know the swells and currents, every inlet and indentation, every tree that clings to the cliff-side.

'I know the gradations of sky and sea, every nuance over the full range of the colour spectrum. I have caught thousands of fish here, and observed many more, photographed them, and followed them to their lairs. I know the subtleties of the bay. I have fished, dived, sailed and swum upon and within it. And over the past nineteen years I have done so in the company of my boy.'

I have known the boy's father for the two decades since I first began coming to the island. Known him as a thinker and an anarchic spirit, tempered by a patience cultivated in his years at sea. I have sat with him in conversation for many hours, drawn by his contemplative nature.

'This is my fault,' he says. 'There are times when I have dived down and not wanted to return. I have wanted the sea to take me, to keep me in its depths. I have had to will myself to resist the temptation, and I infected my boy with the same madness. I should have been the one taken. It was always the two of us. I cannot bear the thought of returning to the boat. The sea is dead for me now.'

He says this as a plain statement of fact, without rancour, without a trace of self-pity. 'Children should bury their parents,' he adds, echoing a universal lament. He sees it all, the nights and days on the bay with his boy, his friend and comrade. He sees the two of them on the boat making its way into the bay, letting out the nets and dropping anchor. He sees the path on which we are now standing from his vantage point on the deck of a boat in the waters far below us, with the boy beside him. He burns with his sorrow.

'I hate the sea,' he says. 'I hate the day I first took my boy on the boats. I hate myself for encouraging the mania that killed him. I will never sail again. I will sell my accursed boat and be done with it.'

Ti na kanoume, ti na kanoume. What can we do, what can we do? *Ola ine tikhe, ola ine tikhe.* All is luck, all is fate. The refrain is a threnody, from the Greek, *threnoidia,* from *threnos,* 'wailing' and *oide* meaning song, a dirge, a lament for the dead. An unashamed keening, a raging against fate. It is the song that comes unbidden when all else fails us. All that is left in the wake of tragedy. All that can be said.

A Chorus of Feet

It wakes me at dawn, the steady rhythm, the percussive beat. It can be heard as I stir from my sleep. It rises from the streets with the aroma of coffee, the clinking of cups, the clash of cutlery and plates. I unfasten the shutters, look out over the rooftops and glimpse the canal at the end of a side street.

The early sun is seeping in, lighting a table strewn with a laptop and notebooks: the tools of my trade. I descend the stairs, stop at the ground-floor café, order a coffee and drink it standing at the crowded counter among Venetians who down their espressos in one hit. When I am done, I join them as they hurry out.

On the pavements I jostle with the crowd. A woman flings open the shutters and pounds the bedding on the windowsill.

Romanian musicians, a fiddler and an accordionist, carry their instruments in search of a busking place. A plump middle-aged woman saunters over a canal bridge. She wears red stilettos, a black mini-skirt and a low-cut red blouse. She strides through the streets, her head held high, her back straight.

Commuters are waiting at canal stations, boarding vaporettos, hailing water taxis and spilling off gangways into streets and piazzas. Goods are being delivered in handcarts and trolleys and on barges and motorised boats. One boat transports a miniature forest of bonsai trees. A second is loaded with winged angels and haloed shepherds bound for the cemetery island of San Michele. A boatman stands at the stern, one hand on the tiller while the other holds a mobile phone to his ear. His workmate lounges on a cushioned wheelbarrow, legs dangling over the sides beside mounds of gravel and cement.

The absence of cars is a leveller, and the city a democracy of feet. I now know that the music I have become a part of is the tread of Venetians on their way to work. The rhythm evokes memories of journeys I have made to Venice over the years and my first approach by boat, a voyage that I owe to a chance encounter in 1974 in Eilat, a Red Sea port.

In the first weeks I had worked as a dishwasher in the kitchen of a beachside resort. My domain was a small space, about two metres wide and three metres in length. I cleaned the machine each morning in readiness for the waiters' assault. They rushed by with the breakfast dishes, and slapped them down on the bench. Mid-morning I wheeled out the garbage. The desert heat slapped my face. Flies crawled over the refuse; the smell of rotting food choked the air.

The kitchen was a hellhole. Tempers were frayed. Cooks squabbled. Fights erupted. During one lunch break, a waiter flew at me without warning, punching and clawing until he was dragged away by workmates. 'Don't worry,' they assured me. 'He runs amok from time to time. Don't look him in the eye and all will be fine.'

I left the kitchen to work on the building sites. It was far better out in the open, the lines of work more clearly defined. My immediate superiors—the carpenters and plumbers, bricklayers and plasterers—were Palestinians. After I had worked with them for a month, they invited me back to their communal house.

I placed my work boots beside a row of boots lined up by the door. On the kitchen shelves were photos of the women and children the men hadn't seen since embarking on their latest work stint. My workmates took out photos from their wallets and laid them on the table: a stone house in Bethlehem, a two-storey home a family once owned in Jaffa, a house in a refugee camp in Jericho, from which they had fled after the Six Day War before settling in an apartment on the West Bank.

For a time I worked in a desert settlement laying foundations for bomb shelters. Late one afternoon I wandered over to a Bedouin camp. Through the flap of a tent I saw a man and his family, seated on rugs for an evening meal. He invited me in and motioned me to sit and eat. 'Schweya, schweya,' the old Bedouin said. 'Slowly. Slowly. Haste is from the devil. In the desert there is no other way.'

Schweya. Schweya. The hills and valleys around Eilat were

scattered with people who were drawn to the fringes: a circle of Japanese hippies who spent their days in a wadi seated in the lotus posture, a retired biologist who set out each dawn on the off chance of locating a rare desert species, and an eighty-year-old pilgrim from Texas who had come to the 'Holy Land' to await the second coming of the Messiah.

Just as I was planning to move on, I exchanged books with a fellow traveller. Thomas Mann's *Death in Venice* had fallen into my hands. It was not the mid-life crisis of the tortured writer Gustav Aschenbach, his weary heart and his fraught search for distraction, which drew me. I was not yet weighed down by ambition, not yet enslaved by a compulsion to produce. Rather it was Mann's description of Aschenbach's approach to Venice by sea that made an impression—the domes and bell towers that rose from the water as if in a dream. And the first sight from the San Marco canal, as Mann put it, of 'the most remarkable of landing places, that blinding composition of fantastic buildings which the Republic lays out before the eyes of approaching seafarers: the soft splendour of the palace, the Bridge of Sighs, on the bank the columns with lion and saint, the advancing, showy flank of the enchanted temple, the glimpse through the archway, and the giant clock.'

As Aschenbach looked on, 'he thought that to reach Venice by land, on the railroad, was like entering a palace from the rear, and that this most unreal of cities should not be approached except as he was now doing, by ship, over the high seas'.

On the travellers' grapevine I learned there was a ferry service from Haifa to Venice. A month later I was on board, moving out on the Mediterranean. The winds of history were charting our course. The boat did not dock, as was the plan, in Cyprus. In recent months the island had been invaded, properties razed and islanders driven from their homes. Settlements lived in for generations were occupied by strangers claiming them as their own. The line between Turkey and Greece was being brutally contested and redrawn. The new border cut through towns and villages, impervious to the pleas of those who had long lived there, those who had worked the fields and vineyards.

The boat dropped anchor in Piraeus the following morning. I had left Athens in November, and in the intervening months the junta had been overthrown. A weight had lifted from the Polis. It could be felt on the streets. The thoroughfares were thronging with strollers, a lightness in their steps.

During my previous stay my Greek appearance and youth had been grounds for suspicion. The city was under the control of soldiers and police. I was harassed many times, had my passport scrutinised, my bags searched. Perhaps I was observed entering the music store that acted as a front for the activities of dissidents whose fellow students, months earlier, had been overrun and killed by army tanks. 'We have no more tears to shed,' whispered the manager of the yards where I had worked building ferro-cement yachts.

From Piraeus the boat cut through the Corinth Canal and turned north along the Ionian coast. Throughout the night a succession of ports drew me back on deck, to the sight of yet another town perched on a steep hillside, houses descending like vines to the waterfront. On each approach, the same dreamlike sequence: the dark outline of mountains, the entrance to the harbour, the boat docking, heaving its bulk to the wharf like a beached whale. Then the boat disgorging cars and travellers, buses and trucks, directed by stevedores and port officials lit by globes hanging from the quayside posts.

In one port a gypsy woman moved among the disembarking passengers selling tissues. A truck driver, oblivious to the commotion, squatted over a primus stove, cooking his meal in a frying pan. Cats sniffed and pawed at luggage, in the vain hope of accessing the food within. I stood on the deck in the anonymity of darkness, witness to feverish welcomes and farewells. Then the entire sequence was re-enacted in reverse: the ropes untied and flung on board, the whale heaving its bulk from the quay, the town lights receding and the wind assuming its sharp bite as the boat returned to the open sea.

Sunrise heralded a full day on the Adriatic. The boat was following the former trade routes of maritime empires. On the starboard side stretched the austere mountains of Albania. Then there were hours at sea beyond sight of land, the boat occasionally moving closer to shore within sight of fortress towns, once on guard against attack on two fronts: the sea and the hinterlands.

The following dawn I was back by the rails. Thomas Mann did not betray me. A damp mist was rising, unveiling the outlying isles. Two hours later, proceeding along the Grand Canal to Piazza San Marco, the landmarks appeared as Mann had described them: the Ducal Palace, the projecting side wing of the basilica, the giant clock and gate tower and the piazza columns topped by lion and saint.

Thirty years later I approached the city by sea a second time. I stood on the deck beside my ten-year-old son. Islets moved towards us, seagulls circled, wheeling and swooping over the deck. And on my son's face, a look of wonder at the scene unfolding: cathedrals and mansions, cupolas and domes, appearing, disappearing. Buildings restored and glowing, others in decay, bruised and flaking, stucco crumbling: Venice suspended like an apparition under a rising sun.

Now, three years later, I walk a city that I have traversed many times. It has been barely a day since my most recent approach, this time by train from Warsaw. During the night I was jolted from sleep several times by border police banging on the compartment door, demanding my passport, shining torches on my belongings and at my face.

Stations whipped by like lanterns. Countries appeared and vanished. The announcements of stationmasters broke into my dreams like brazen strangers. I opened my eyes to the serrated outlines of mountain ranges. Or was I dreaming, imposing what I had seen by day on the passing darkness: the forested slopes beneath the snowline, the ravines and valleys, the alpine hamlets.

I stirred from my restless sleep at dawn, as the train was passing over the causeway from the mainland. Venice is the terminus to an entire continent, Santa Lucia Station, the final stop. *Schweya. Schweya.* Haste is from the devil. I stepped out with the milling throng into the forecourt and descended the stone steps to the canals.

By sunrise the following morning, the Venetian chorus had

fully reclaimed me. It accompanies me under archways and over bridges, through culs-de-sac and alleys and into unexpected courtyards, past hanging gardens, dwellings with misshapen chimneys, and water, always water, and boatmen calling, their voices clear and transparent in the carless city.

Workshops are being unlocked. Artisans are at work in the confined spaces they had taken leave of the previous night: shoe-makers and upholsterers, lithographers, glass blowers, ceramicists, jewellers and mask makers. Shops are being opened: patisseries and cafés, photographer's studios, tourist bookstores and empo-riums trading in Venetian crafts and artefacts.

Yet, as on my previous visits, I find myself returning like a homing pigeon to one particular enclave in the northwest corner of the city, far from the landmark glories of Piazza San Marco. I stop at a hotel where I had once stayed, and climb the stairs to reception. And he is there as I had last seen him, standing behind the counter.

'You can see me because I am not dead,' he says, as if continuing a spiel we had left off when we last met. 'And if I am dead, how can you see me?'

At seventy, Signor Marcello retains his sardonic air. His hair is grey and receding, his cheeks a drinker's red. He wears an open-necked white shirt and a pair of grey trousers. His belly is a gourmet's paunch. His gaze is direct and wary, and on his face is the wry smile I had come to know so well during a previous stay here.

'You want a nice coat? You have to pay. You want a beautiful woman? You have to pay. You want to live in a beautiful city? You have to pay. So my good friend, why should it be any different for a hotel?'

'I don't need a hotel,' I say. 'I have dropped in to pay my respects.'

'I know what you are up to,' he says, finally recognising me. 'All you care for is a story. All writers are thieves and scavengers. Will you give me a share of the royalties? Eh? You want to do business you have to pay. You want information you have to pay. You want a story you have to pay. So why should it be any different with my tale?'

Yet he obliges and adds flesh to the bones of a story he had begun when we first met. His father was born in Budapest into a Jewish family and had worked, as a young man, in the hotel business. He arrived in Venice in 1920 with his Austrian-born Catholic wife, and worked his way up from kitchenhand to waiter, then from receptionist to manager of the hotel.

He bowed and scraped, grinned and nodded, stood to attention, hauled trunks and suitcases, scoured and polished. He tended lifts, fetched newspapers, knocked on doors tray in hand, lit cigars on the lips of strangers and cleaned the mess of departing guests. He performed his duty without fail, and with utmost courtesy. He fathered two sons and inched his way up the hierarchy, and had finally become the director of a hotel on the Grand Canal.

The building rose from damp foundations on the approach to Piazza San Marco. The sights that had drawn Aschenbach out of his torpor were Marcello's father's daily reality. After years of labour he could now afford a little time to indulge them. He stood on the uppermost balcony and allowed himself a moment's reflection. Below him, vaporettos and gondolas, steamers and barges moved by in a hypnotic parade.

He did not mind that Venice's glory days were long over. In fact he preferred it this way, preferred the loss of imperial ambition and the live-for-the-day mentality of its hardened citizens. He understood, as someone who had spent a lifetime tending to the needs of those accustomed to wealth and dominance, that empires are built on power and servitude.

He belonged to the backrooms, to those who maintained the show. Those who set up the props, vacuumed the dressing rooms, stoked the boilers, scrubbed the curtains and readied the city for yet another day of spectacle. He knew the rear side of the peacock: the warehouses, loading docks, factories and chemical works, the city's engine rooms. He knew the cunning of the traders and the scams of the boatmen who had so annoyed Aschenbach.

And he knew of the darker history: the secret tunnels and cells within the Doge's Palace, the trials that had taken place in the empire's heyday. He had seen the routes of the prisoners before they were hauled before their inquisitors, their journeys to damnation. He knew the travails of those who questioned the prevailing order, knew that no empire could thrive without its armies of the night, its clandestine networks of spies and informers.

He knew the contrast between the visible splendours and the hidden horrors, between the turrets and arcades, the marbled hallways and corridors, the sumptuous halls where the Council of State once presided, and the apparatus of violence hidden away behind walled passages and padlocked doors. He knew of the torture chambers, the iron collars clamped around necks, the slow strangulation by garrotte.

He knew Venice from the bottom up, and loved it for what it was. Yet he did not know that the city was not done with imperial ambitions.

The Nazis entered Venice in 1943. 'It was spared from being bombed,' Signor Marcello tells me, 'because the Germans were spread throughout the city. The hotel was commandeered for Nazi officials. Fortunately, the commandant took a liking to my father. After all, we are a family of handsome men. Take a good look. I bear a remarkable resemblance to Marcello Mastroianni, no?'

He pauses, glances at his reflection in the foyer mirrors and runs a comb through his hair, strategically rearranging the thin strands.

'The commandant offered my father a bone,' he says. 'Convert to the Catholic faith and your family will not be put on the train. The word "train" made my father shudder. He was aware of the rumours of slave labour camps and worse. Hotel workers are the most discreet of eavesdroppers. We know what is what ahead of time.

'My father converted. What choice did he have? Eh, my good friend? You want to stand in judgment? You want to assume the superior air of the intellectual, the holier-than-thou observer? I know how it is. I know the way you and your kind think. I know that you see yourself as above the dirt that most of us have to grovel in.

'You have not had to face questions of life and death, my friend. If you want your children to grow up in one piece, you have to pay. If you want to stay alive, you have to pay. If you want to save your family, you have to grab the bone that is thrown to you. This is what my father taught me, and this is how it is.

'Unfortunately my fellow countrymen did not fare so well. I may look like an ignoramus, but I know my history. The Jews of Venice were rounded up and deported. The first train left some time in November 1943. Forgive me. I am not certain of the exact date. I do know, however, that the last train departed eight months later, on August 17.

'Yes, my friend, I know what took place as my father chewed on the bone that was thrown to him, and as we, who depended on him, sucked on the marrow. Of the two hundred and two Venetian Jews deported, just eight returned. Unbelievable, no?

'And through it all I have remained a Catholic. What was the point of changing back? If it would save my life and the life of my children I would be whatever you wished: a pagan, an idol worshipper, a devotee of any god. Let them all fight each other and preach salvation. It is all the same to me, as long as I am left in peace. This is how it is.'

The words accompany me as I descend the stairs. 'This is how it is.' Pronounced as a statement of defiance. I imagine the scene as I continue my walk. Marcello's father feigning salutes, clicking his heels, nodding at Nazi banners while in a parallel world, in another part of the city, his fellow Jews were being driven to the station, to the death camps.

Just one bridge and a tunnel, and I am there, in that

particular maze of streets I have come to know so well. The sun is still low, the alleys and canals shaded. Here and there a glint of light plays upon the water's surface. Underwear and bedspreads, sheets and towels hang on lines strung between balconies over narrow waterways. The multi-storey tenements on either side are all but touching. The lower reaches are skirted with damp and patches of stucco peeled back to brickwork. Small boats are tied at tiny landings jutting from weathered walls that resemble the colourless scales of dead fish. Pigeons fly down from leaden rooftops, their wing-beats amplified in the narrow confines.

Despite its former might, Venice is a brittle city, built upon shifting foundations: mud flats, drained marshes, swamps and sandbars. This enclave and its pockmarked beauty lure me; its grim romance holds me captive. It feeds my obsession with the darker recesses of history. I scribble the key dates and episodes in my notebooks. And this is what I write:

In 1516, the Venetian Republic's ruling council debated whether Jews should be allowed to remain in the city. The dilemma they faced was this: how to contain the 'sworn enemies of Christ' who would pollute their religion, without losing their services as physicians and intermediaries between Christians and Muslims, as traders and as moneylenders, a task they were allowed since Christians were forbidden to charge interest.

Thus the first ghetto was born, in the streets I am now walking. The deal was this: the city's Jews would be confined to a dirty, polluted island, linked to the rest of Venice by three bridges. The island was the former site of an iron foundry where, in the fourteenth century, metal was cast to make cannons.

By day, the inhabitants, identified by circular yellow badges and yellow scarves, were allowed to ply their trade on the Rialto, but two hours after sunset in winter and one hour after sunset in summer the three drawbridges were raised, the guardian gates padlocked. Guards stood at the gates and patrolled the surrounding canals in boats to ensure that the enemies of Christ would not creep out and contaminate the populace.

The word ghetto derives from this site, from the Italian *getto* meaning 'casting' or from the Venetian, meaning 'foundry'. Confined within a small space, the inhabitants expanded upwards, building vertical additions, houses up to six storeys high, far higher than buildings in the city at large, with tiny rooms, low ceilings and prayer houses on the upper floors crowned with miniature cupolas, restrained and understated.

'This is how it is,' I hear Signor Marcello saying. You want to survive, do not draw attention to yourself. You want to live, make do with what you've got. You want to protect your children? You must create a labyrinth of escape routes, secret doors and tunnels, passageways, false walls.

The ghetto was isolated, yet its isolation protected its residents. And they took their chances. They created a mini civilisation, a city within the city, invested it with its own myths, its subtle glories. Some came to see it as a biblical camp of the Hebrews, a miniature Jerusalem, a way stop for scholars and pilgrims. There were five synagogues, one each for the German, Italian, Spanish, French and Levantine communities that settled here, each community with its history of dispossession, its journey in search of a new way to scrape a living.

They made the ghetto a centre of culture, complete with literary salons, an academy of music, a theatre, and a place of commerce with inns for merchants and travellers. The main street was lined with bookshops, second-hand dealers, printing works, pawnbrokers and banks, tailors' workshops. Venetians were drawn to the district as soon as the gates were unlocked at dawn.

In time the boundary between ghetto and city became more fluid. Ghetto physicians, lawyers, merchants and scholars assumed a prominent place in the daily affairs of the Republic. At night, young men stole out of the ghetto to party in the city. The gates were more easily scaled, the guards more willing to turn a blind eye.

The ghetto's fortunes rose and plummeted in tandem with the fortunes of Venice. During the 1700s it fell into bankruptcy, mirroring the economic and political decline of the Republic. In 1797, Napoleon's troops brought an end to the Venetian Republic. The ghetto gates were demolished and in time its residents were granted equal rights. The enclave remained the centre of the Jewish community, its buildings subject to cycles of disrepair and restoration. Then it all ended with the Nazi occupation, the robotic beat of soldiers, herding families onto trains bound for death.

Then I see him. Signor Marcello walks slowly, glances around him, as if not wishing to be noticed. In the sunlight, away from reception, his familiar territory, he looks more aged, less certain. He is carrying a bouquet of yellow flowers. I follow him at a distance. At this hour, the narrow alleys induce a sense of the clandestine, a play of hide-and-seek between sun and shadow. There is a furtiveness about the signor. He steps into the shell-shaped central Campo del Ghetto Nuovo.

Signor Marcello walks the length of the piazza to the memorial bas-relief panels beside the Casa di Riposa building. He pauses from time to time, to catch his breath and his bearing. When he reaches the memorial wall, he lays the flowers at the base of the bronze bas relief depicting the last train bound for annihilation.

He stands, head bowed for several minutes, while I watch just out of his sight. We are alone. The piazza is deserted. The morning rays slink through the side streets and break out into the open. The bronze panels glint in the sunlight.

Signor's flowers lie by the wall in a blaze of yellow. The rays play upon his polished black shoes. Only now do I become aware of the shift in tempo. The chorus of feet has ceased. The beat is gone, and the rhythm has dissipated. The square is silent.

The Partisan's Song

They were the first to hear the poem that became the anthem. No one present that day could have known how famous the song would become, that it would be sung by ghetto fighters and by partisans in forest hideouts on the eve of battle, and, to this day, at memorial services of survivors worldwide.

It was in late April 1943 in a dimly lit cellar beneath the Vilna ghetto. There were four present: Phillip Maisel and his twin sister Bella, Meishke, the streetwise union leader, and the poet Hirsh Glik or Hirshke as his friends called him. They were seated at a table, a single candle was burning, and Hirshke read aloud two poems he had recently completed. The first, 'Quiet the Night', portrayed the daring exploits of a partisan girl.

The second poem, 'Never Say', would become renowned

as the partisan's song, the de facto hymn of the resistance. Bella questioned the words in the first verse. She asked, 'Why did you use the word *poyk*? Why, *a poyk ton unzer trot*, the drum beat of our steps? What does it mean?'

Hirshke did not answer. Once he wrote a poem he never changed a word. The music was yet to come, but those present heard the poems fully formed, word for word as they are sung to this day.

I first heard the partisan's song as a young boy in the 1950s, performed at a memorial evening as I stood with a community of elders. In fact many were not so old. They ranged in age from about thirty or so, but the stories they carried within them made them seem older. Paradoxically, as the years went by, this conferred upon them a sort of agelessness. The impact of what had befallen them, what they had lived through, remained the constant, regardless of their physical ageing.

The song was sung at the end of the evening, as an anthem. The audience rose to its feet to sing it. From the opening lines the hall resounded with voices. The lyrics were an exclamation, an emphatic statement.

> *Never say you are on your last way*
> *When blue days are concealed by skies of grey*
> *The hour we have longed for is surely near*
> *With the drumbeat of our steps: We are here!*

The song marked the end of the ceremony, an end to

lamentations and remembrances. It signalled a transition back to reality. I stood between my elders, dwarfed by their presence, overwhelmed by the raw strength of their numbers, and their lust for survival.

> *From green palm lands to lands white with snow*
> *We are coming with our anguish and our woe.*
> *And where a spurt of our blood will fall*
> *Will sprout our courage, our unyielding will*

Brutal reality and hope alternated in equal measure. Even then I understood that the song was a miracle of poetry: an act of defiance, wrought from a time of terror, yet somehow infused with spirit. Unnerving imagery tempered with lightness.

> *The morning sun will gild our present day*
> *And our yesterdays will vanish with our foe*
> *Yet if the sun delays and in the east remains*
> *Through generations this song will be passed on.*

By the fourth verse, the anthem appeared endless, and this is how I wanted it. I was a child among fighters, protected and secure in their presence. I was being inducted into their secret. Within this gathering of survivors the bonds remained strong, and the sense of comradeship was palpable.

> *The song is written with blood, and not with lead*
> *It's not a song by a bird in free flight overhead*

It holds a people trapped between falling walls
The song is sung with weapons in our hands

At some indefinable point, our age differences dissolved and the distinction between generations vanished. I was a part of the collective, an accomplice in an act of restoration. All that existed was a communion of voices submerged in one voice, harking back to the first verse, for a final word, a restatement of purpose.

Never say you are on your last way
When blue days are concealed by skies of grey
The hour we have longed for is surely near
With the drumbeat of our steps: We are here!

By the song's end, the night had been fully restored to the poets. We filed out of the hall in silence. At this time of year the air was crisp, tinged with intimations of winter. Many of those present lived within walking distance of the hall. Located on the edge of the inner city, the neighbourhood was an intimate enclave where survivors had regrouped and begun the ascent back to normality.

We walked beneath glowing street lamps, past the homes of friends, across median strips planted with palms and poplars, along familiar back lanes with fences shrouded in darkness. We were half a world away from the scenes of the crime, yet on this night we were being stalked by its shadow. We walked the four blocks home in near silence, and if we did speak, we did so in whispers.

Phillip Maisel sits by the lounge-room table on an autumn morning in 2010. He leans towards me, his elbows on the lacquered surface. The previous evening we had sat at the kitchen table late into the night. Now that I've heard the bare bones of his story, I am eager to hear it in full.

He is small, but fit and agile for a man of eighty-seven. He pauses from time to time, lifts his head and looks into the distance in search of the memory. His English, which he acquired quite late in life, is precise and measured, with a hint of the syntax of the other languages he has acquired over his lifetime. He selects each sentence with care.

'Hirshke was a quiet boy,' he says, 'very shy, unassuming. And we were friends. It is strange. When you are young you don't need much to become close friends. We met in 1941 during the Soviet occupation. I will tell you something very interesting. We were very leftish, and this is what brought us together. The story is like this.

'Before the war Hirshke was living in the poorest part of Vilna, a suburb called Snipiszki. His father was dealing with second-hand clothes and scrap metal. He could not afford a wagon, and did his business on foot. As far as I remember, Hirshke had one sister and two brothers, and they were all musical. They were the poorest of the poor, and their poverty deepened when their father died.

'When we first met, Hirshke was working in a shop selling stationery. I was also working in such a shop. We were members of the same trade union. We attended meetings every Thursday. I was young and a romantic, and meeting someone who was a real poet was very exciting.

'In Vilna there is a river called Wilja, and after the meetings we were usually going for a walk on the riverbank. I wrote poetry that was published in a newsletter. So I was some sort of a poet.' Phillip sits back, folds his arms and laughs contemplating his literary talents.

'Hirshke was a real poet, but I felt we had something in common in the way we saw life. You may call it strange, but this was the way we saw things. He was expressive, a true artist. He had his own language, his own selection of words that were unique to him.

'He was about my height, five foot four, and neatly dressed. I see him by my side, strolling by the Wilja. But I do not see the river. I see myself listening, attentive, talking very little. I was learning from him, even though he was just two years older. Yet he was only twenty when we met. He had dreamy eyes, but he was actually more practical than me. He had faced more poverty in his life. I came from a comparatively well-off family.

'When Hirshke was looking at you, you could see something was happening inside him. He was always thinking, always searching for meaning. This is pure speculation, but I assume he was creating a new poem. I admired him for his ability to express himself in poetry. A poem is like music. It says more than the words that appear on the paper.

'One of the things I marvelled over, but did not comprehend, was how he was able to create an entire poem in his mind before he wrote it down. He carried it around in him. He allowed it to grow. But once he wrote it down he would never change it, not even one word.

'Then in autumn 1941 the Germans occupied Vilna and everything changed. They would snatch people in the street and take them to prison, and from there, to be shot in Ponary. It was like this: Ponary was located in the forest on the outskirts of Vilna. When the Russians had occupied the city in the previous two years, they started to build storage facilities in Ponary for oil tanks. They dug deep trenches to house the tanks, but when the Germans took over they used the pits as mass graves for the murdered.

'The killings started straight away. The Germans were picking up Jews from the streets and taking them to Lukiszki prison and, from there, in trucks to Ponary. When they caught someone in the street it was for one of two reasons: for work, or to kill them.

'We lived in constant fear. Many thousands were killed before the ghetto was created. That is why some of us were relieved when the ghetto was established. At least there seemed to be a stop to the random abductions, but it did not take long before we realised this made little difference. The murder and the maltreatment continued.

'For a time I lost direct contact with Hirshke. I was living in a different part of the ghetto. Meishke was our go-between. He had been the secretary of our trade union. He kept up with the members and he always knew what was happening. He was a close friend of Hirshke. There was a rumour he was in love with Hirshke's sister, who was very beautiful.

'Who was Meishke? He was a man who lost his father when he was young. His mother had to support the family. He never had a proper suit in his life. He was always wearing second-hand clothes that were a little bit too big, oversized jackets, long trousers. He was very skinny. Before the German occupation he joined the Komsomol, the youth organisation of the Communist party.

'I will tell you something interesting. His father died well before the war, and to support the family his mother bought and sold chickens. She would walk to a village several kilometres from Vilna, purchase a pair of chickens and return to the city to sell them at the market. She would use the profit she made to feed her family, then she would walk back to the village and buy two more chickens, and so on.

'Can you imagine such poverty? At a meeting of the Komsomol, a party apparatchik asked, "What is your mother doing for a living?" Meishke told him she sold chickens at the market. "Ah, so your mother is a business woman," said the apparatchik. "That makes you the bourgeois son of a trader." Meishke was thrown out of the Komsomol, but he would still come to meetings. No one minded. The rules were set in Moscow, and we were far away.

'To tell the truth, Meishke did not care. He took things as they came. There was so much injustice in the world it was no surprise to him to find some injustice in the Komsomol. He was not formally educated, but he was very clever, quick-witted and aware of world affairs. He had his own way of seeing things, his own sense of humour.

'He worked in a food shop during the Soviet occupation. There was a cat that lay in the shop all day, but it could not be left there overnight. Meishke would get him out of the shop by enticing him with the tail of a herring.' Phillip laughs. 'I was waiting for him after work and he would be dangling a herring in front of a cat.

'When we were driven into the ghetto, Meishke was the one who knew what was going on. He was a catalyst, the one who brought people together. Through him I would find out what was happening to Hirshke. He told me that he was working in the forests. Hirshke was one of a group of people that the Germans sent from the ghetto to a place called Rzesza to collect turf.

'You see, turf is formed by decaying vegetation in the swamps and marshes. After many years it solidifies, and can be burned as fuel. Hirshke's work brigade was cutting it out of the forest floor and letting it dry out. It is very hard work. The turf is full of water, very heavy. They would have to wade in the peat bogs. In Lithuania the climate is cold and wet. Every few months they would come to the ghetto to get some food supplies, and then return to their camp in the forests.

'Meishke told me when Hirshke was back in the ghetto, and we would meet, at most for about thirty minutes. We were exhausted from work and lack of food. We were all starving. We lacked basic necessities. We used newspaper to make a fire in the woodstove to cook our meals. I would meet Hirshke in the street and have time only for a quick conversation. We talked about who was alive, who had died and who had joined the ghetto underground.

'At our places of work, members of the resistance tried to find things that could be used as weapons. I was working in a garage where I learned to be an automotive electrician. I managed to scavenge flexible steel coils that had been used to protect the truck ignition systems. We thought perhaps we could use them to fight the Germans.

'One meeting with Hirshke was a special occasion. He said, "I have just written two poems. I want to read them to you." So we went to the cellar under the building where I was living, or shall we say, existing. There was nowhere else to go; we were crowded into every little space, in tiny rooms, in attics and garrets.

'The cellar entrance was inside, not far from the stairway, hidden by bricks. After the ghetto was established we called the cellars bunkers. The four of us went down together. We lit a candle, sat at the table and Hirshke read the poems.'

Phillip closes his eyes and puts his hands to his forehead. 'Actually we sat on boxes,' he says, 'and I doubt it was a real table. It was some kind of wooden box. The cellar was large: say, the size of about three rooms. It was dark, a place for hiding from the roundups. There was a hole in the wall that connected it to the next cellar. During the German raids, when they came to get us to take us to the forest to kill us, we were hiding in the cellars. Everything was uncertain. Anything could happen at any time. We were always on the lookout for danger.

'Hirshke was a shy boy, but when he read his poems he changed. He did not raise his voice but you could feel his passion. When you were with him you could sense an inner life, that he was keeping something back. Do you get it? But when he read the two poems it was different. He was alive.

'Hirshke wrote his poems in 1943, in late April, shortly after the outbreak of the Warsaw Ghetto Uprising. It has been said the uprising inspired him. I had no idea when he read the poems that one of them would become so important. But this is the strange thing: the conditions were so primitive, so dangerous, but you still had the capacity to express yourself, to write such poems. Even more so than usual.'

On the wall behind Phillip is a silkscreen painting of two geishas. It is large, two by two and a half metres. A fold divides it in the middle. The older geisha is showing the younger woman how to hold a fan. She observes the pupil with full attention. On her face there is a hint of gentle approval. The young geisha is focused on the fan, which she holds, delicately poised, in her fingers.

Everything is balanced and mannered. The figures embody an age-old ritual between teacher and pupil. Their relationship hints at a vast history, an enduring tradition. The figures are caught in a moment that suggests centuries.

The parallels between the painting and our conversations are uncanny. There is something of the teacher–student rapport between Phillip, the older man, handing over the story, and me, the listener, eager to receive it. The young geisha has taken hold of the fan and I have taken hold of the story, which like the fan is delicately poised. At this point it hangs in the balance.

'I will tell you something even more interesting,' says Phillip. 'I know how Hirshke died. To my knowledge, no one knows exactly what happened. Some say he escaped from a work camp in Estonia and was killed fighting with the partisans. Others say he escaped in 1944 when the Russians were closing in and was probably executed by Germans. All that is known for certain is that he vanished. Then, unexpectedly, here in Melbourne, not so long ago, I discovered what happened.'

Phillip stops, puts his hand to his chin, and contemplates the story. Like Hirshke in composing his poems, he allows his words to take shape before he gives them to me. When he resumes he chooses them with great care, acutely aware of their gravity.

In the ensuing hours I come to understand his logic, the method in his detours and repetitions. It is not only the story, but the way it is told, that conveys the meaning. The detours are critical to knowing Hirshke, his dreamy nature, the process by which he composed his poems, and the means of his passing.

'The story is like this. On the first of September 1943, early in the morning, German troops and their Estonian collaborators surrounded the Vilna Ghetto. Inside, we already knew that something was about to happen, a round-up, perhaps the final massacres in Ponary. The time had come. The resistance put out a call for the fighters to get ready for battle.

'Most of the ghetto inmates went into hiding in the cellars and bunkers. There were two battalions of fighters. One went to the Jewish hospital and barricaded themselves inside with a few guns, a handful of homemade grenades and an array of improvised weapons.

'I belonged to battalion number two. Our weapons were primitive and untested. We had made them in secret workshops. We had between one and two hundred electric globes. The pin of the globe was broken off, the bulb filled with battery acid and resealed with lead. Each of us took two globes. We gathered in a courtyard and waited for the Estonians to enter.

'Imagine a big courtyard with two entrances, one at the front and the second at the back, and we are facing one entrance. Suddenly the Estonian soldiers appear in both entrances armed with machineguns, and force us to march to the front of the yard. It was autumn. I had the globes in my overcoat pocket. I decided that if I were going to die, I would die with dignity. So I put my hands in my pocket and walked slowly. But the Estonians just passed me and left me behind. Nothing happened.

'I was at the rear of the group. I saw an open window and jumped through it. In the corner of the room there was a wardrobe and that was where I hid. I stayed until I heard the noise dying down. I could hear the footsteps of the Estonians on the cobblestones, the steps of one of them entering the room, searching, and I heard him saying, "Nobody here."

'I waited for twenty minutes and decided to go to the hospital where some of the fighters were assembled. I sneaked through the streets, knocked on the door, and the people inside said, "The door is barricaded. We are not going to open it."

'Not far from the front door, in the courtyard, there was a pile of wood for the hospital heating.' Phillip draws a diagram in my notebook. He sketches the square courtyard, with apartment buildings on two sides, the hospital on the third, and a gate between buildings on the remaining side. He draws the wood stacked in front of the hospital.

'The pile was approximately two metres high. I climbed up,

hid myself on top of the wood, and waited. An Estonian soldier walked into the yard through the gate and he was heading in my direction. I found an axe, and I calculated that from where I was hiding, above the pile, I would be able to split the head of the soldier. I could easily lean over and hit him as he walked by. But I did not do it, because in reprisal they would kill a few hundred Jews. And you would not believe it. A little girl, nicely dressed, strangely enough, was walking towards the Estonian from a doorway on the opposite side of the square with an axe in her hand. The soldier grabbed the axe and threw it away. He gave the girl a gentle kick in the behind, and told her to go home. So you see, I had spared the life of someone who still had some human feelings.

'A few minutes passed and I walked out to see what was happening. I saw a policeman walking in the street. I showed him my work pass, but he said, "Today it is not valid. I'm arresting you." He took me to the gate of the ghetto where the Germans were waiting with trucks. They searched me and they found the light bulbs. They threw them onto the cobblestones and none of them even broke. They were useless.' Phillip laughs, shrugs his shoulders, and gestures as if to say, we were hopeless fools, deluded in our hopes for our homemade weapons.

'The Germans pushed me onto a truck, and the convoy moved in the direction of the train station. Because I had worked in the German Army car repair unit in the ghetto, I knew where the battery was lodged under the floor of the truck. There were about twenty people on board and I suggested that we should try to get to the battery and disable the truck. None of them agreed. They were afraid we would all get shot.

'We came to the station and they put us in cattle wagons, eighty in each. They counted us loudly, from one to eighty, and they said: "If one of you escapes, all of you will be killed." One of my schoolmates had run off to the forests some time ago to join the partisans. That day he had come back to recruit some people. He was discovered and shot on the spot, beside our wagon. I saw it.

'They gave each of us a loaf of bread and some water, put a bucket in the corner for our basic needs, and at about four o'clock the train left in the direction of Ponary. We all expected to be shot, but we passed the forest and travelled further north. The people in the wagon, fearing reprisals, made sure no one tried to escape.

'We travelled for three days and came to a transit camp in Estonia called Auvere. We were there for three or four hours. We eat some soup, and we are sent to another camp.'

Phillip has slipped into the present tense. He is unaware of the transition. From now on, he alternates between present and past, between the reliving and the remembrance. He is both present and distant, both at the table and in the slave-labour camps of Estonia, and he is taking me with him. From time to time my eyes stray to the geishas. Somehow, they too seem far removed yet fully present.

'There are no barracks, only tents,' says Phillip, 'with about thirty people to a tent, and, as it happens, in my tent they were all young people involved in the resistance. So we were all thinking about how to escape.

'My job is to build the barracks, and my dream is that a truck would break down and I would be asked to fix it. And it happened. One day, two Germans came to our tent leader and asked for motor mechanics. The tent leader asked me if I could change a tyre and he sent me away with other fellows who would be working in the garage.

'This saved my life because in the garage we are not exposed to the cold, and not exposed to so much animosity from the guards. Instead we received a degree of respect because of our skills. What does it mean a degree of respect? They would some-times leave behind the crust of the bread, as extra food. Do you get it? This is all relative. We had been elevated to the status of half human, and we stayed alive.

'And because of my work, I ran into Hirshke. Can you believe it? It was as if we were destined to meet again. This is the story. I was working in the mobile garage and I moved from one camp to another, all over Estonia, repairing trucks and cars for the German army. At night they would put me in the nearest hard-labour camp.'

Phillip stops, forever conscious of the need to extract the signifi-cance of the story. 'Yes, being an automotive electrician saved my life. In the Vilna ghetto we understood this. Your life depended on how useful you were to the Germans. They issued certificates, which provided you with a degree of security. Back in 1942, a friend of my father's worked in a ghetto garage repairing cars, and they required an automotive electrician. So my father decided I should become one. I had studied some physics at school. It was my only training. I knew little about cars. I told them I was an electrician.

'My first job was to sweep the floor. The floor was earth, so I could sweep all day. When my foreman was at lunch, I experimented with the starter motors, generators and distributors, trying to see how they worked, how they were built. The other workers in the garage showed me how different electrical parts were working in a car.

'This is interesting. In the ghetto there was a library that contained a lot of books about electric circuits in cars, electric motors. I learned from those books. I began collecting the old parts that were to be thrown out and, by tinkering, taught myself how to repair them. So I became very useful. And in Estonia, I made sure I would remain useful.

'Estonia is very cold and the Germans had large diesel trucks. The engines were too big to turn over with a crank handle, so during the night they had to put a fire under the truck so that the engine would be warm enough for the starter motor to turn over in the morning.

'I discovered the reason why the starter motor did not work well. Because of the cold weather, the magnetic force was too weak to close the gap between the two contacts in the relay that operated the starter motor. So I decreased the gap.

'Again I proved to be useful. But I also knew that when it got hot the starter could burn out. So in the longer term, what I was doing was a form of sabotage. It was a kind of balance. I did what had to be done to survive, but I found a way to subvert it. After all, those I served were murdering my people.'

Phillip laughs. His pleasure in his subtle acts of subversion remains with him. He props his elbows on the table, draws in his shoulders, and touches his fingers together. Then, reminded of his purpose, he returns to the central thread, his meeting with Hirshke.

'On one of my journeys we were staying two nights in a camp called Goldfilz. The inmates in the camp were returning from work. They were walking slowly, exhausted and hungry. Among them I see Hirsh Glik. I discovered that Hirshke's fighting unit in the ghetto was captured, and he had been deported to Estonia not long after I was.

'Why Estonia? The Germans had discovered shale rock from which you could extract oil. They were desperate for fuel and there was a labour shortage, so they used the Jews of Vilna to produce it. Thousands of able-bodied men from the Vilna Ghetto were spared the massacres in Ponary so that they could mine shale in Estonia.

'The instant I saw Hirshke was a bright moment. Such things are relative. We lived with uncertainty. We did not know what would happen to us in the next hour. You are in a dark tunnel and the light is flickering far, far away, and you do not know for how long it will flicker, and you hope that you will eventually reach it. It is hard to describe.

'I saw that Hirshke was the same person, still dreamy. Malnutrition creates a certain psychological state. You saw in a prisoner's eyes that he was disturbed, but Hirshke had a steady look. He wasn't defeated.

'The first conversation between us was very short, but once you were in the camp at night you could move freely among the inmates. So when he finished eating I asked him, "Hirshke, how can I help you?"

'Hirshke replied, "People respect me for the songs I write, and sometimes they allow me to have the better part of the soup from the bottom of the pot. But I have one problem. I do not have a spoon."

'Again you must understand what does it mean, "respect". When people were in the queue for the soup, because they admired him, they would not push or hit Hirshke. They allowed him to retain his dignity. If you lost your dignity, you lost your will to live. Believe me, this is very important.

'It was so easy to lose your dignity. In the camp there were certain jobs that made it more likely. The worst job was to carry the wooden troughs full of human waste. Little bits would spill over you and you stank. My word of honour, one of the worst nights I ever had was when I was ordered to do this job. The snow was slippery and I had to carry the troughs. I stank for days.

'In the camps food was always on your mind. Hirshke did not ask for a bit of bread, he asked for a spoon. That was a good sign. He was not thinking like a starving person concerned only with immediate survival. Not only did I have a spoon, I had one with a sharpened edge so that it could be used as a knife. I would cut my daily ration of bread in half in the morning when I received it. I ate the second half in the evening with the soup we were getting when we were returning from work. I gave Hirshke the spoon.

'For him it was a treasure. For me it wasn't a big deal. I knew that in a few days I would organise another spoon. We were friends. Believe me, in conditions like that friendship was a matter of life and death.'

Phillip leans forward, and emphasises the point with his clenched fists. He allows the thought to settle before resuming. 'After I gave him the spoon I asked him, "What else do you need?" "Something you can't help me with," he replied instantly. "I need freedom."

'He said this in a manner of a bird in a cage. As if it was the deepest innermost desire existing in that moment. He said it with the same feeling he expressed in the cellar when he read the two poems. His entire being, his deepest longing, was in that moment. It made such an impression on me. I thought: "This person needs freedom like one needs fresh air."'

I look at the painting. It is filling out, beginning to convey a more expansive story. The two geishas are elaborately dressed. The blue-grey fan is the bond between them. A second fan lies fully opened on the floor in front of the older geisha. Her clothing is more ornate than her pupil's; a shawl is draped over her shoulders.

The younger geisha is in the foreground. She wears a crimson kimono with a floral pattern. She occupies a little more space. She will have the greater responsibility since she is the student and will have to carry on the tradition. As yet, she remains inno-cent. The pressure appears mild. She is a geisha in training. There is serenity in the painting, and an exquisite stillness between the women.

I return my attention to Phillip. Between us too there is space born out of stillness, reinforced by the quiet of suburbia on a weekday morning. There is time for the story to quietly unfold, and for both the teller and listener to contemplate its meanings.

'What did the camps teach us?' Phillip asks, and in reply he says, 'The basic difference between right and wrong. The good people became better and, unfortunately, the bad became worse. The strongest impulse in a person is to survive. Then it is important how you survive. And how you survive determines what sort of a person you are.

'This is why for many years I assumed that Hirshke died by attempting to attain freedom, knowing he may lose his life in trying. And then, by chance, I found out what happened. In 1993 I interviewed a fellow in Melbourne called Samuel Drabkin. I was collecting testimonials for the Holocaust Centre. It became my new obsession, after my passion for collecting oriental and primitive artworks.

'You see, a person must have a purpose to live a long life, and my purpose is to work in the Holocaust Centre. I am in charge of the testimonies department. When I tutor students, I direct them to the materials suitable to their studies.'

Again Phillip is weighing his words, aligning them with his speculations. 'It is teaching young people that I love. I really believe in it. It is my real purpose. And in fulfilling it, along comes this fellow Drabkin.

'He was also from Vilna and, at a certain point while he was giving his testimony, I realised that he and Hirshke were on the same transport to Estonia. They spent their first days in the transit camp Auvere, and were then sent to Goldfilz. This is life. Unpredictable. Something you never expected to find, and suddenly you discover what had happened to a friend.

'I made another appointment with him, to record the exact details. The story he told is something like this. It was in 1944. Autumn. The prisoners were returning from the forests where they were cutting wood to be used in the mines. They were a group of about forty.

'Suddenly they are surrounded by Estonian guards. The prisoners knew there was something unusual happening back in the camp. As they approached, they saw the German Commandant standing by the window of the barrack drinking vodka, and they heard the sound of shooting.

'The prisoners were passing a toilet block, a wooden building with a big window. They ran into the building and climbed out the window. They reached a wire fence, broke through the wire and started running to the forest, everyone in different directions, and the guards were shooting.

'About fourteen people survived. Some were captured by the guards and brought back to camp. Drabkin had four brothers with him in the camp. The youngest disappeared when they were running for the forest and he assumed he was killed. His name was Isaac.

'In fact he did survive. Drabkin met him after the war. He was an eyewitness and what he saw is now on record in the Holocaust Centre. Isaac said he saw Hirshke shot and killed by the guards as he was running.'

I cannot yet let go of Hirshke. I am burdened by the gravity of the story and the need to honour the nuances. Something eludes me. The story remains incomplete. I return to Phillip's house weeks later, and step out of the car to the quiet of a suburban morning.

Minutes later, Phillip and I are standing before the geisha silkscreen. He points out details only an educated eye can appreciate. 'The painting is a few hundred years old,' he says, 'maybe much older. The partition between the two screens is a means of protecting the work from earthquakes. When a quake strikes, the painting can be quickly taken down and folded.'

Phillip delights in his knowledge. He ushers me closer and points to the older geisha. 'You see? She is wearing an *obi*, a wide sash over the waist of her kimono. It is an important part of her attire. It shows her higher status. Her pupil is not yet entitled to it.

'Artworks hanging on the wall are rare in Japan. The Japanese prefer to have a view of the garden, the living landscape framed by a large window. Look carefully,' Phillip says, bending forward, gently touching the silk. 'You will see that the screen is made up of small squares, each about five inches square, glued together to produce the larger material.

'Japanese artists are very sensitive. They are trying to say things that are very important to them. Their work is rich in symbols. I am not an artist. I cannot express such things as an artist. It is even more difficult to express subtle things in words. Only the poets really know how to do it. You see, this is why I loved Hirshke.'

We return to the table, to the same positions we had during our previous conversation. The silkscreen of the geishas remains the backdrop. I ask Phillip about the incident that first drew me here: the night of the reading in the cellar, and the poems.

'Yes,' says Phillip. 'I think that the song about the partisan girl, "Quiet the Night", was the more important of the two poems for Hirshke at the time he wrote them. It was the first one he read. He was a fighter, a member of the partisan movement, but he was not a killer. Everyone loved Hirshke. I have not heard or read one unkind word about him. He was a dreamer, he loved life, he loved people, and I think he loved the partisan girl.'

'Her name was Vitke Kempner. At the time that Hirshke wrote the poem she was already in the forest, blowing up trains with explosives. Together with two companions, she blew up a German military transport carrying two hundred soldiers on the outskirts of Vilna.

'Then she walked three days and nights with wounded legs and feet back to the ghetto. It was the first of many acts of sabotage by the partisans of Vilna. Hirshke honoured the deed in his poem, and he himself selected the captivating music.

'It is said that Vitke had a lover in the forest. As far as I know, for Hirshke it was love at a distance. All he could do was write the poems, and this one was both about her and about resistance in the form of the partisan girl. You see what it was.'

I am beginning to see, to fill in the picture. On the surface, there is a cellar, a single candle. And beneath the surface, the flickering flame of love, even amid the brutality and slaughter. Now I see the picture anew: the four friends huddled around a makeshift table, and, at the helm, a poet in hell, clinging to his humanity, extracting fragments of poetry from the horror. The two poems are inseparable: partisan girl and partisan anthem: love and defiance, longing and rage, acting in tandem. Together they complete the picture.

The Ancient Mariner

When she was born her mother was upset she had not given birth to a boy. Her father said, 'I am not upset. I am glad I have a daughter.' He named her Amal, meaning hope, and he took her to many places in his dark green Morris. Every Friday, the day of rest, he drove her to the Tigris, to walk along the banks of the river. As they walked he sang to her from the repertoire of Umm Khultum, the grand diva of Arabic music.

One morning as father and daughter were strolling by the Tigris they came upon a gathering of people dressed in black, weeping. 'What happened to these people?' Amal asked. 'They have lost their son to the river and they are waiting for his body to rise to the surface,' her father replied. 'Bodies can float,' he said.

'In the ocean, many times I wanted to die,' Amal would tell me years later. 'I was waiting for the angel of death, but I remembered what my father told me and I held onto the body of a woman. And I heard music. I heard Umm Khultum, and the songs my father sang when we walked by the Tigris. Maybe this saved me.'

I first met Amal in July 2002. She appeared distracted, and anguished. Her gaze was directed at me and beyond, to places far distant. In time I came to understand that it took in the streets of Baghdad, the banks of the Tigris, her perilous escapes in the dead of night, black seas beneath black skies, and the moment the boat sank, Friday, October 19 2001. 'At ten past three in the afternoon,' she said. 'I know because the watches stopped at this time.'

It was the first of many times I heard Amal recount her tale, fuelled by a desperate need which increased as she approached her final months: 'My brother, when I die, you must tell my story, and the story of what happened to the people who died in the ocean. Tell the people about my father, and the songs he sang when we walked along the Tigris.

'Tell the people I love music, I love colour, I love movies. Tell them I love Baghdad, but when I see it on the television, when I see the bombs falling, when I see what they do to the people, I do not know my city. It has a different colour. I do not know that colour.'

Five years after her death I am fulfilling my promise. Yet each time I sit down to write, anxiety rises for fear I will not do the story justice, will not find the words that convey the terror and beauty of Amal's telling, the fire in her eyes, the look of incredulity and wonder she retained even until the last days before she died, four years after I first heard her tell it.

I recall the many places I heard her recount it, in the various dwellings she lived in, across the northern suburbs of the city where the new communities have settled, within walking distance of stores stocked with fashionable hijabs and emporiums boasting Ottoman treasures from Turkey, shops with businesses named after ancient kingdoms—the Phoenician Café, the Euphrates hairstylist—miniature replicas of Baghdad and Beirut, Istanbul and Ankara.

I recall the public gatherings at which I heard Amal speak: the town halls, schools, mosques and churches, at a memorial service in the national capital, and in a packed cathedral in Sydney where she embraced a fellow survivor. Oblivious to the audience, the two women were weeping and swaying, and Amal was saying, 'I am still in the water with the dying!' And the night she stood on stage at the Melbourne Town Hall before an audience of two thousand, her headscarf glowing in the spotlight, her black robes all but lost to the darkness, and her expression of childish wonder as she prefaced her umpteenth telling by saying, 'When I was a child, my dream was to become a singer, an actor. I dreamed that one day I would become famous. Today I received the Oscar!'

I reflect on the talks she delivered within hours of completing yet another course of chemotherapy, the night she pleaded with nurses and doctors to allow her temporary leave from her hospital bed to speak, as arranged, at a memorial meeting. And the late night phone calls, Amal ringing because she dreaded the dreams that awaited her when she succumbed to sleep, fearing her nightly return to the ocean: 'My brother, I am not like I was before. I cannot sleep. I am afraid I will see the ocean. I think I lost something in the ocean. I want to go back to the ocean. I want to ask the ocean, what did I lose? Is there something the ocean has to tell me?'

She says that every night she sleeps on the water. She is alone, and she cannot breathe, and there are people shouting, 'Get back, get back, it's dangerous, you are going to drown, you are going to die,' and she puts her hand out to prevent herself from sinking, and wakes covered in perspiration. She welcomes the pre-dawn birdsong, the greying light seeping through the blinds, her return to the routines of the living.

She says there are nights when she gets out of bed, dresses, steps outside, and wanders the streets to prevent her dreams from returning. She tells me of her late afternoon forays, riding the trains to the city. She sits apart, but she is among people, listening to a walkman, to music, always music. Leaving the train at Flinders Street Station and descending the steps to the river to walk its banks as she once walked beside the Tigris.

She cannot stop thinking about the tragedy, cannot erase the images. She says she wants to paint what happened in the ocean, to paint the corpse that saved her, paint the children asleep on the water, paint the mother and newborn baby still attached by the umbilical cord asleep upon the ocean. She has epic vistas in mind: paintings she has seen of the sinking *Titanic*, panoramas in the manner of Delacroix, Picasso's *Guernica*.

Amal knew of such works because her husband, Abbas, owned a gallery in Baghdad selling imported posters of classical artworks and paintings of Baghdad streets, iconic places. She sketched the scene many times in preparation for a canvas. She was desperate to get it right, to portray the individual people, the men, women and children choking on water, the mayhem and horror, the boat going under. 'My brother, I lost something in the ocean. I want to find it. Maybe I will find it in a painting.'

Now I too am anxious to get Amal's story right, to find the words that will capture her eloquence, and convey the story with the clarity and poetic vision that was evident from our very first meeting, in the winter of 2002, within weeks of her arrival in Melbourne—in a neighbourhood centre, a refuge named Becharre House after the birthplace of Khalil Gibran, the peripatetic poet, a fitting setting for our first encounter.

The people of the city are at work, the traffic snarls long over. A quiet has settled on the streets. Young mothers wheel prams and strollers. School children walk hand in hand, setting out on an excursion. The morning radiates the blessed ordinariness that Amal yearned for in her years of turmoil.

She sits by a table in black robes and black hijab. A short, rotund woman, she leans forward, her palms facing upwards, fingers curling, imploring. Her hand gestures are expansive, her amber eyes alight with expectation and gentle fury, and she is telling me:

'When the boat went down, I saw everything. I was like a camera. I cannot forget anything. I want people to know what happened. Maybe that is why I am alive, to tell the story of the boat, to tell about the children and their dreams, and the women and their dreams, to tell of the men and what happened to them in my country. And why the Iraqi people want to escape, why we had to take this boat to save our lives, to save our families. Maybe this is why I did not die in the ocean.

'The motor stopped and some people tried to fix it. Suddenly the water came up and the women screamed, "We are going to die! We are going to die!" They could not believe it. I looked down and saw the water touch my legs, and I did not know where was my son. I looked down at the water, and it came up quickly. It felt like someone was touching my heart and pushing me down in the water.

'I didn't shout, I didn't say anything. The boat went down quickly, quickly. Quickly. I closed my eyes and when I opened them I saw that I was in the ocean, and I saw there were children under the water with me. I cannot swim, and because I cannot swim I did not breathe, and because I did not breathe I did not swallow water, and maybe this is why I am still living. And when I came up to the surface, the doors of hell opened.

'My brother, you can't imagine. I saw children drinking the sea, and they were shouting and going under. I heard one woman saying, "God, I am going to die now," one man crying, "My wife die, my daughter die." Someone is shouting, "Oh my family, I lose all my family," and one woman is screaming, "I lose my children, I lose my husband, I do not want to stay alive, I lose everything." And my friend is saying, "Please, God help me, help my little son, he is going to die, please help my baby." And another friend is shouting, "I lose all my daughters. God help me, I lose all my daughters."

'And I said, "Oh God, this is hell. What has happened to us?" I said, "I can't die. I must fight. I am a mother. I must fight because I have a son in the water, and a son who is waiting for me in Iran, and they are going to lose their future. I must fight because I have a daughter who lives in Jordan with her husband and four children. I must fight because I want to hold my father's hand and walk with him by the Tigris."

'I fought, but I did not shout. I looked at the people. I saw everything. I saw the people's eyes and they were frightened. I saw one woman floating with her baby. The cord was not broken, and the baby was sleeping on the water. This woman was from Iran and she was seven months pregnant. She told me before we left Sumatra that her husband is in Australia. He has a temporary visa, and she must go in the boat to see him. She is going to follow him, and she feels happy, but when the boat sank I saw her dead body in the water.

'Another woman, she was sixteen years old, she also was pregnant, and she also gave birth in the ocean. Now she and the baby are sleeping on the water. Maybe they are dreaming. Maybe I am dreaming.

'And I see the children. I know them from the hotel in Jakarta where we were waiting. The children look fresh. They look like angels. They look like birds, like they are going to fly on the water. One girl, she is eleven years old, and she is lying on the ocean, and her eyes talk to me. They are saying, "What crime have I done?" And I say, "Oh poor, beautiful girl," and I see her falling asleep on the ocean.

'Then one big wave carried me away and I started to swallow water. I thought I was going to die, and another wave pushed me under. I didn't want to die. I pushed down on the ocean with my hands and I came up out of the water, and when I came up I saw my son, Amjed. He is sixteen years old and he was frightened, but I cannot come to him. He was touching a piece of wood, and when he saw me he started to cry, and he said, "Mum, we are going to die."

'We can't believe it. We think it is a bad dream. He said, "Mum, please come and save me." He said, "Mum, I can't swim." He said, "Mum, please forgive me, maybe I have done something bad to you." He said, "Please come closer, I want to kiss you." It is hard for me to talk about this, because he is young, and he is my son, and I am his mother.

'In that moment I saw a woman coming up from the ocean. She was wearing a life jacket, and she was dead. And I remembered in Baghdad, when I was a little girl, and I was walking with my father by the Tigris, we saw many people sitting by the water, crying and waiting for the body to come up to the surface. "Bodies can float," my father told me, and in the ocean I remembered what he told me, and I held onto the woman with one hand, and I swam with the other hand to my son, Amjed.

'He took off her life jacket and he put it on me, and he saved me, he saved my life. He kissed me, and a big wave pushed me away, and he shouted: "Mum, I love you, I am sorry we are going to die," and he said, "Goodbye Mum. Maybe I will see you in paradise."

'A wave took me away from my son and he disappeared, and

the wave carried me to other people. They were fighting for their lives, and they were shouting, "God help us. God help us." There were children in the water, and they could not say anything. They could not talk, but their eyes looked to me for help. They knew they were going to die. I could not believe what happened to them. I did not shout. I just looked at the people. I was like a camera, and many people shouted, "God help us. God help us." There was bread and biscuits, bottles of water and gasoline, pieces of boat, suitcases and oranges swimming on the water, and the people were crying, "God help us. God help us."

'After one hour, everything became quiet. I thought there was no one alive. I was alone, and there was nothing, only the sky and the water, and the dead woman. I asked, "Why am I still alive?" And I answered, "Because I am going to tell the world what happened to us. I am going to talk about the children and their dreams. I am going to talk about the men and women who wanted to make a new life for their families."

'I talked to the dead woman. I told her, "My sister, please forgive me. Maybe I am hurting you. Maybe it is not nice to touch your body," and I asked her, "What did you lose in the ocean? Did you lose your husband? Did you lose your children?" I asked her, "Did you lose your soul?" She was a young woman and I could not look at her face. I felt shy. I wanted her to forgive me. The rain was falling and the ocean was angry. I talked with the dead woman and I asked her, "My sister, please stay with me. My sister, please forgive me."

'The night was falling, and it was dark, and I could not see my hand. Dead bodies and fish were touching me. I smelled gasoline, and I saw a black island spraying water. I swam to the island and I saw it was a whale, not an island. Then I saw lights moving over the water. I thought maybe there is another island, and I started to swim to the lights.

'One light was touching my hand and touching the dead woman, then the light was touching the tail of a shark, and the shark was swimming around me. I smelled of gasoline. Maybe this is why the shark went away and did not eat the people in the water.

'I was not alone. There were other people in the ocean. The light was sweeping over them, and they were holding pieces of wood and they were swimming to the lights. And they were crying, "Help, help, please save us!" I came close to the lights and I saw it was not an island. It was a boat. The young men were swimming and they were saying, "Follow us. We are going to the boats. They are going to save us," and I tried to paddle with my hand, to swim faster.

'There were three boats, two bigger and one smaller. I thought they were going to save us. The light was shining in my eyes and we were shouting and screaming. "Help. Help. Please, help us!" I heard the voices of the people in the water, and I heard the horn of the ships. I got closer, closer to the boats and I shouted, "Help! Help! Please, help us." I thought they were coming to save me. One man had a whistle, but no one on the ship wanted to hear him.

'I tried for two hours, but they did not save us. They did not save anyone. Some people let go of the wood. They felt hopeless. The boats disappeared and I was alone on the ocean. It was cold and dark and raining, and there was only sky and water. I looked to the sky. I wanted to see the angel of death. I wanted him to take my soul. I wanted the angel of death to end this, and take me from the ocean to the sky, to lift me from the water.'

Amal breaks off and glances around her, disoriented. The strain of the telling has tired her. She wants to talk for a while of other things, her love for her son Amjed, and for her older son, Ahmed, who is waiting in Iran, and the married daughter, who left Iraq years ago and lives in Jordan. She wants to tell me about her daughter's four children. Her tension eases as she speaks, her voice softens. She is relieved to be away from the ocean.

We meet again weeks later, in the flat she has recently moved to. Amal walks from the lounge room to the kitchen to tend to her cooking, and returns to tell me that in Iraq, every Friday, it was her habit to make *dolma*, the dish she is now serving: chopped tomato and minced lamb stuffed in vine leaves, seasoned with paprika, cumin powder, lemon juice and pepper. She is a restless woman, eager to express her passions. She delivers baklava and cardamom tea, and puts on a CD of Umm Khultum in live performance.

The music evokes *Alf layla wa-layla*, the *One Thousand Nights and One Night*, and tales of her beloved Baghdad, which stands on the Tigris four hundred and fifty kilometres north of where it meets the Euphrates on a plain once known as the Fertile Crescent, a region that archaeologists contend was the cradle of civilisation. And it takes Amal to that once-upon-a-time when life was good and her family content. This is how she recalls it decades later in a city far distant, coloured by time and nostalgia, and the gloss of childhood.

She lived in a suburb of the old city in a house with six rooms, a garage and garden. The house was full of banter. Her brothers grew their hair long, inspired by the Beatles, and put on false moustaches in imitation of Charlie Chaplin, whose old movies were in fashion, and became avid fans of *Some Like It Hot, Saturday Night Fever*. It was that treasured era when her father took her out on the day of rest to the banks of the Tigris.

'I walked with my father every Friday,' Amal tells me, 'and sometimes the people gave us fresh fish from the river. We walked every Thursday night too. There were many people near the water. There was a big garden and a long beach. You could eat anything. You could sit there with your family. We had a good life. We did not need anything. My father was an engineer and he liked to take us driving in his Morris. We drove to many places. I had eight brothers and one sister, and I had many dreams. Maybe I would become a doctor, an actress, a singer, maybe a lawyer.

'I finished high school and I studied in a business school. Then I worked in the Central Bank of Iraq, eight good years when I loved my job. Every morning when I signed my name I was alive. I was working. It was a good life for me. My husband, Abbas, had three shops. He was building a good business. He sold pictures of famous artists, singers and film stars. He had Iraqi artists who were making for him paintings of Baghdad, old mosques and palaces, the famous places of my city.

'But the bad times came and there was war between Iraq and

Iran. We were fighting against our brothers and sisters. It was not safe. There was no food and no medicine. There was no school. We did not use oil. We did not have meat. We used to say our food is "air food", like nothing.

'My brother, I want people to know why we escaped from Iraq, and why we came on the boat. I want people to know why the people took their children, why I took my son and went on the ocean. Why we wanted our freedom.'

Amal is emphatic, her voice urgent. She returns to the rise of Saddam Hussein and the dark times, which she says began with the outbreak of the war against Iran in 1980. 'Baghdad started to become a dangerous place and my husband had to go into the army. They told him, "You must go to war," and they told me, "You must leave your job and stay home with your children."

'I looked after my daughter, my baby sons and my husband. I looked after my mother and father, and my brothers. We did not need to make war with anybody. Before the war we had everything: we had jobs, we had children. I was upset when I left the bank, because I had to fight to get that job.

'The war with Iran lasted ten years, then for one year we rested. I told my husband, "Maybe we are lucky. Maybe we can do something. Maybe we can have a new life now." But Saddam made another war, with Kuwait, and after this war there was no food, no medicine. There was nothing, nothing in my country. I had lost my job, and now I started to lose my family.

'Saddam killed my brother, Sa'ad, because Sa'ad did not want to fight with Kuwait. My brother said, "The people in Kuwait are my brothers." After they killed him, the police called my father and said, "Come and take your son's body." We had to get his body and clean it for the burial. When we looked at him we saw that his clothes were filled with blood, and they were torn and dirty.

'My father took me away. He did not want me to see this, but one of my brothers stayed and he found a letter in Sa'ad's jacket. It said: "Please take care of my children. I say goodbye to the earth, and say welcome to my God." My mother told me "Come and say goodbye to your brother." I went inside and I saw they had put some white clothes on his body.

'Another brother, Bahir, was killed when Iraq was fighting against America. He was twenty years old. He worked in Basra, in the Iraqi security, and an American bomb killed him. I lost two of my brothers, and I lost my uncle and cousin. It looked like we were losing all the young men in our family, and then, in 1991, the police killed my husband's brother, Saleh. He was fighting in the uprising against Saddam in Karbala, and the military caught him and killed him. We never saw his body.

'In 1995, another brother of my husband disappeared. He wanted to rise up against Saddam, and when they caught him they killed him and the police came looking for my husband. They arrested him and put him in jail and they asked him, "Do you know something about your brother?" They asked him why his brother did this bad thing. They asked them why he didn't like this regime. My husband said he did not know anything about this. He did not know his brother had joined these people.

'They kept Abbas in prison for fifty-five days and Saddam's police tortured him with electricity. They asked many questions and after he was sent home, they told him they wanted to talk to him again. My husband told me, "They are going to kill me. We must be ready to escape."

'One day he called me, and he said, "I can't come home." I asked him, "Why can't you come home?" And he said, "I can't tell you now." He told me he was hiding with a friend, and he was calling me from his friend's phone. Saddam's police knew his number. They knew everything. Abbas told me, "Be careful." Everyone was scared. No one knew who was a friend, who was the enemy.

'I slept with my children and at midnight I heard people knocking on the door. We were scared, my children they were scared so much. When we opened the door the police asked me, "Where is your husband?" I told them I don't know. They searched the house. They looked everywhere. The police were angry because they did not find him. They broke furniture, they threw things on the ground, and they were calling me bad names and shouting, and my children were crying.

'And the men told me, "You must come to the police station." I told them, "I don't know where my husband is." I told them, "I argued with him, and he did not return home." They took me to the police station and they asked me more questions. They kept me there until morning.

'The next day, I left home. I took my children and some clothes and we escaped. I was frightened. I went to my family's house and I stayed with them. When we saw police we were afraid. My son Amjed told me, "I have bad dreams about policemen."

'My husband and my son Ahmed had escaped to Iran. They

paid some smugglers and they escaped over the mountains. Abbas rang me from Iran and told me we must be ready. He told me I must take Amjed and escape. The smuggler came and said, "Don't bring furniture. Don't bring your clothes. Don't bring photos. Don't bring anything." I went outside with Amjed, where the smuggler was waiting, and I said goodbye to my family.

'My mother was very sick. She had a stroke and she could not walk. She needed medicine and she needed special food, but in Baghdad there was no medicine, there was no food. I was very sorry I had to leave her. My mother told me, "Please don't go. Please stay with me." I told her, "I can't. I must look for my children's future. I must do this for them."

'It was dark when I left the house, and I looked at the homes when we were driving. The people inside were sleeping, and I asked, "Will I have a home again?" And I asked, "Will I see my family?" I asked, "Can I save my children's future?"'

Limbo, the scriptures say, is a state worse than death. In mediaeval times limbo was defined as a netherworld suspended between hell and redemption, a realm for lost souls in search of a home. Limbo comes from the Latin, *limin,* pertaining to the threshold, or *limbus,* meaning 'hem' or 'border', as of a garment. In literary usage it means a state of restraint, of confinement and exclusion, in its extreme, as equivalent to prison. To be in limbo is to be consigned to live on the margins, in no-man's-land, with the future tantalisingly close yet agonisingly out of reach.

When Amal left her parents' home for the final time and was driven through the streets of Baghdad, she left the city she had lived in for fifty years. She took leave of her foundations. All she had known was slipping away beneath the wheels of the car that drove her from the city into limbo, north towards the mountains of Kurdistan, bypassing police checkpoints.

Settlements rose like ghostly apparitions, and dissolved back into darkness. Amal was plagued by the thought that Saddam's shadow would overtake them before they reached their destination, the city of Sulaimaniya in Iraqi Kurdistan, within reach of the Iranian border, and north of the ill-fated Halabja, the town that Saddam had bombarded with chemicals one decade earlier, killing many thousands, leaving the dead and dying scattered over the streets and squares, gutters and alleys. The victims lay where they fell, the dying retching and vomiting, the dead bleached of colour, contorted in agony.

For Amal and Amjed, Sulaimaniya was a sanctuary, even though they were confined to one small room, a sharp contrast to the spacious surrounds they had known in Baghdad. The room had no gas, no electricity, no running water, but it was a haven nevertheless in which they could take stock, and gather strength for the onward journey.

Years later, while under anaesthetic in a Melbourne hospital, as doctors operated to remove her cancer, Amal dreamed she was sitting in a cave in the northern Iraqi mountains. It was a beautiful cave and she was dressed in new white clothing. Everything appeared white. She wanted to remain there, to rest, to surrender. Her sons came to her and interrupted her peace.

They said, "You must leave now! Hurry! It's time to go. We

must run!" Amal resisted. She was reluctant to forsake the calm of the cave. Her sons grabbed hold of her hands and dragged her out. As she was pulled clear the dream ended, and Amal woke up and realised the operation was over.

The dream rekindled Amal's memory. She tells me of her onward journey from Sulaimaniya when I visit her in hospital a few days later. Her husband and older son had returned from Iran to join them because they did not want Amal and her younger son to undertake the hazardous border crossing without them.

Days later the family joined a convoy of three other families, and left the city at the fall of darkness. They were driven north by smugglers and came to a stop short of the border. They moved on by foot, a party of twelve, climbing towards the higher slopes of the mountains. They were guided onto a narrow path as rain began falling. One smuggler led the way and two brought up the rear. They stumbled over rocks and exposed roots, and forded a river; the water rose to their upper bodies. They scrambled over mountain passes, descended and ascended, leaning on staffs they had cut from branches.

They walked fast to avoid the Iraqi police patrolling the borders. In the near distance could be heard the howling of wolves and the movements of bears and foxes. As the night sky thinned out to the first signs of dawn, the smugglers shouted, "Run! Run!"

'I told them I cannot run,' says Amal. 'They said, "You must run." I tried hard to run. Soon after we began to run the smugglers said, "You do not have to run. You are in Iran now." I turned my face to Iraq. I said goodbye to Baghdad, and I said goodbye to my family, to my friends. My brother, you can't imagine. In that moment I knew I would never again see my country.'

And years later, after Amal's death, as I write the story, her voice takes hold and works its way back into my consciousness. It is with me as I go about my daily business, and returns with greater force when I resume writing. Something is niggling me, something about her voice, its intonations and cadences, the repetitions, its musicality.

I make my way to Sydney Road, the main thoroughfare in the northern suburbs, to the 'Platinum Desert', a shop that specialises in Arabic music. I ask if they stock Umm Khultum. 'She is still loved many years after her passing,' says Omar, the Lebanese musician who runs the business. 'She is still our best-selling artist. We have CDs that were recorded in the 1940s through to the last ones before her death in the 1970s.'

He sorts through the shelves and returns with a selection. Over four million people attended her funeral in Cairo, he tells me. It was the largest single gathering of people ever recorded in history. She was mourned throughout the Middle East and the people still revere her.

Omar grew up in Beirut listening to Umm Khultum. When he was young he idolised her, and as a musician he still turns to her for inspiration. He chooses a CD and plays it for me. The sense of melodrama is apparent from the opening bars of the prelude. The instrumentation is a synthesis of western and eastern: violins and cellos, double bass, violas, the oud and zither, with tambourine rhythms. The prelude paves the way for Umm Khultum's entrance. She is greeted by a roar from the audience.

People loved her for her unrestrained emotion and the epic stories she told in her songs, tales of loss and longing and the fortunes of ill-fated lovers. She improvised, paraphrased, dramatised and adapted, while remaining true to the tradition. Each performance was an act of renewal, building from quiet beginnings, increasing in intensity, and culminating, for the performer and audience, in an exalted state known as *tarab*.

In Umm Khultum's voice I hear Amal's. In the rhythms, I discern the tempo of Amal's telling. In its repetitions, I come to understand Amal's recounting as an incantation, which the ancients saw as a way of raising the dead, and of restoring them to the living. In the rising tension, the build-up of emotion, I hear Amal willing her tales to their limits, conveying her truth through gesture and emotion, inducing in her listeners a state of enchantment.

I hear her voice intensifying, ebbing and flowing to and from the state of *tarab*, rising in a succession of waves before receding back to an interlude, while she regained her resolve and nerve before proceeding with the next ascent in the telling.

'My brother, I want the people to know why I left Iraq, and why I wanted to come to Australia. I want to tell them that when I escaped over the mountains and came to Iran, I began to hear about Australia. Many Iraqi people who escaped were talking about Australia. They said there is a way to go there, they said the smugglers can take us. They said that Australia is a democratic country.

'I started to have a dream about Australia. I dreamed my children could go to school there. When they lost their school, they were still young and I worried for them. Now we had a new dream and I must fight to go to Australia. I thought that when I arrived in Australia all my problems would be over.

'But the money was not enough for us, only enough for my husband. Abbas went alone. He flew by plane to Kuala Lumpur, and went by boat to Sumatra, and then he flew to Jakarta. When he arrived in Jakarta he called me and told me he was upset because he had left me alone with our sons. He said we must believe that one day he is going to save us.

'He called again and told me that he had seen the ocean, and he was very scared. He told me that many people had disappeared in the ocean, and I told him, "Don't go on the ocean. Come back to Iran." He said, "I can't go back now. I must do something for my children."

'I talked to him again in December, and then for a long time I didn't hear from him. I was scared that the boat had sunk and I had lost my husband, but after two months he called again and he said he is in Woomera Detention Centre. He is in the desert, and he does not know what is going to happen to him.

'I was scared because I lived with my two boys and we had nothing. We lived in a small room. I cooked in that room. Our clothes smelled like that room. We felt hopeless in that room. After eight months my husband called again and he told me that they had given him a visa, a temporary visa. He was not allowed to come back to see us, and he was not allowed to bring us.

'Amjed and Ahmed were upset. They said, "Mum, you told us you are going to save us." I phoned my husband and I told him we are going to follow him. He said, "Don't come, it is dangerous in the boat." He told me, "I am scared. Maybe you will die in the ocean." He told me, "Wait. One day I will be a citizen, and then you can come to Australia."

'I told him I can't wait. I told him, "I must come even if it is dangerous." I told him, "Waiting and waiting is like death. We are slowly dying." He sent me some money and he said, "Use this money to eat, use the money to buy clothes and, if you like, you can rent a nice home and stay there, but don't come. It is very dangerous."

'I didn't buy clothes with this money. I kept the money, and I bought passports. I wanted to buy tickets, but they were very expensive. I did not have enough for three tickets. I did not know what to do. I am a mother. I could not decide which son to take. My older son Ahmed said to me, "Mum, don't feel upset, please go with Amjed, but don't forget me. One day I will follow you."

'I promised Ahmed I am going to save him, but I was very upset. When I had my two sons, and when we went out together, they would walk with me one on each side, and they would hold my hands. They were my wings. How could I fly with only one wing?

'It is very hard for me to remember how I looked at Ahmed's face and said goodbye to him. He said, "Mum don't forget me." He said, "Mum, take care of yourself, and take care of my brother. Mum, I am going to miss you." When the aeroplane went up, my heart was with my Ahmed. And my younger son Amjed felt sick because he had taken the place of his brother.

'When we left I had just one bag with some tins of tuna and vegetables, and Amjed laughed. He said, "The bag is empty, we have nothing." At eleven o'clock in the night we arrived in Kuala Lumpur, and there were many smugglers waiting for us at the airport. The smugglers were fighting over us. They said, "Come with me. Come with me." We chose one and he took us to the hotel. He told us there was only one way to go to Australia. First we must go by boat to Indonesia.

'We stayed in the hotel for three days, then the smuggler said, "Tomorrow you must take the boat to Sumatra." He said, "Take your bag and come with me." We went by taxi and we arrived in a jungle. There was nobody there. There was no food, and nowhere to sleep, no cover. There was only one dirty toilet.

'The next day a boat came. We travelled in the night. There were many women and children. The boat was no good. It was small and it was crowded, and they put some wood over us to hide us, and we could not move, we could not breathe. We stayed one day in that boat. It was very dangerous. The boat stopped in Sumatra and we still had to find our way to Jakarta. A smuggler told us it is a long way to Jakarta. He said it is better to go by aeroplane, and it is cheap, only eighty dollars.

'We bought a ticket and flew to Jakarta, where we stayed in a hotel called the Villa Amelia. We were waiting for a boat to Australia. We talked to a smuggler, Abu Quassey. He was from Egypt. He said he had a strong boat. He said it had everything, and we trusted him. He gave us a big hope, a big dream. We gave him money for the boat. We trusted him because his face was nice. He was like a brother.

'We lived with many Iraqi people, many women and children who had fathers and husbands in Australia. They all had a dream of Australia. The children talked to Abu Quassey and they were very happy. He told them, "In Australia they are going to say welcome to you." He said, "They are going to help you." He said, "You are going to have a good home." He said many beautiful things.

'The children played in a tiny garden, and my room looked over this garden. They woke up very early and they started to run and shout. I got out of bed and left my room, and I said, "Why did you wake me up early? Please, I want to sleep, I feel tired."

'They said, "Please auntie, come and tell us a story." They started to ask me about Australia. They asked, "Have you visited Australia before?" And I told them no. And they asked, "What do you think Australia looks like," and I told them, "It looks like paradise."

'One boy, his name is Sajjad, asked me, "Do you think when I arrive in Australia I will have a PlayStation?" I told him, "Yes, you are going to have a PlayStation." He asked me, "Do you think I am going to be happy?" I told him there is no Saddam in Australia. I told him, "You are going to be safe there. You are going to be happy."

'The children had special dreams. One girl, Alia, told me that when she was a little girl, she played with candles on her birthday and her legs were burnt. She told me that in Australia she is going to have plastic surgery and have beautiful legs, and buy beautiful clothes, and she is going to tell her friends, "Look at me, I have a nice body."

'The children drew many pictures of the ocean. They drew pictures of boats, they drew fish and dolphins, and they drew flowers. They told me, "I want to go to school. I want to meet my father, because I have not seen him for three years." They thought the boat would bring them happiness.

'When we made a deal with Abu Quassey, he said he would be ready after one week, maybe one month, but we waited for a long time. We waited and waited. One day I was watching TV and I saw many buildings burning in New York, and I asked my friends, "What happened? What's wrong?" And they told me al-Qaeda did this. I was very upset about what happened to the people on September 11, and I was frightened because maybe they would say it was our fault.

'We ate, we breathed, we were alive, but we were not happy. The people's money was gone, and they borrowed money from the mosque, and Abu Quassey was not happy because we did not have enough money. He cared only for the money.'

'On October 16, the smugglers took us by bus from Jakarta to Sumatra Island. We went in five buses. No one could see us. There were black curtains on the windows. They took us to a port and at night they put the buses on a ferry. The ferry took us from Java to Sumatra, and the buses took us to some place like a motel. The smugglers told us we are going to go on the boat tomorrow. They told us we had a big boat and it had everything: a radio, a satellite, life jackets, food and water, and bathrooms. They told us we were very lucky.

'On the last day I did not have any food. Many people tried to make some food. They made bread and soup and they gave me some bread. When I ate this bread I remembered the Iraqi people. In 1991 there was no food in Baghdad. I remembered my mother. When she became sick, there was no medicine for her. She died when I was in Iran. And when she died, she had nothing.

'That night I had a dream. I saw my mother. She told me, "Come, I want to show you something." She touched my hand and she took me to a room. The whole room was my brother's coffin, my brother Sa'ad who was killed by Saddam. The room was filled with ice and water. I asked my mother, "Why is there so much ice, so much water?"

'She did not answer. I asked her, "Please tell me what happened." I felt sick. She touched my hand and took me to a bed. I lay down on this bed and I asked her, "Mother, what do you want to tell me?" It was dark and she was holding someone's hand, my son Amjed's hand, and she pushed him to me. Amjed hugged me, and he fell asleep beside me.

'Then the smugglers were shouting, "Wake up! Wake up! We are going now. Hurry! We are leaving!" They woke me from the dream. I did not know then what my dream meant. I did not know that my mother's soul had come to tell me I will be saved, and that my son will be saved. She told me everything. She told me this coffin was not for us. This coffin was for the people travelling with us, and the ice was covering their bodies. I did not understand. I did not know that my mother's soul had come to tell me we are going to have an accident.

'The smugglers took us to a beach. It was one o'clock in the morning. When we saw the boat on the water, I couldn't believe it. None of the people could believe it. The boat was not big enough for us. It was maybe twenty metres long. There were four hundred and twenty people for this boat. My brother, you can't imagine.

'Abu Quassey said, "First I will take just the women and children." They took us in a small boat from the beach, twenty-five people at a time. Maybe they were afraid the men would not get onto the boat when they saw it. What could the women say? It was night, it was dark, and nobody could say anything.

'Believe me, when we reached the boat, I knew it would not arrive safely. When I stepped on board, I told myself, "This boat will not arrive anywhere." Somebody said, "Maybe there is another boat waiting for us?" When the men arrived they were angry and shouting, but the smugglers said, "Quickly! Quickly! Maybe the police will come and catch you. We must leave quickly."

'When the boat was moving we were very hungry, but we couldn't eat because we were sick and frightened. The smugglers told many lies. They told us the boat had a radio, but it did not work. They told us we are going to have so much food, but we didn't find anything, just bread and water.

'The people started to shout, "We don't want to go in this boat. We want to go back to Jakarta." After some hours we saw some islands, and a small boat came close to us and some people jumped on the boat. I told my son, "I want to go with these people. I don't want to stay in this boat." My son went to look for our bag, and when he came back it was too late to catch the small boat.

'We were very upset and one man told me, "Don't think

about this. You don't have any money. If you go back to Jakarta, maybe immigration is going to put you in jail and you are going to lose all hope." I told myself, "This man tells the truth." And I said to myself, "I must pray, I must ask God, please help us. Please help us.'"

Umm Khultum's CD is playing as I drive about the city. Her voice is rising. It is a supplication, an entreaty. It evokes Amal, her urgent walk as she rushed about on errands. Amal as she stood on the Melbourne Town Hall stage, dwarfed by the ornate walls, the tiered balconies and the massive organ, which all vanished and gave way to the ocean, as Amal commenced yet another telling. And it evokes encounters I had all but forgotten, yielding unexpected details.

On the morning of the fourth anniversary of the sinking, I met Amal at Melbourne airport to catch a flight to Canberra for a memorial service. The service was to be attended by survivors. 'My brother, I am tired. I could not sleep all night. I could not stop thinking, where were we four years ago, at this time? Where were we in the middle of the night, fifteen hours before the sinking?

'I got out of bed, made a cup of tea, closed my eyes, and I remembered. It was raining, and the ocean was angry. Our boat went up and down, up and down into the water. Everyone was screaming, everyone was shouting, "My God, please help us!" We were sick. We couldn't eat. We couldn't drink water.

'After midnight, the wind became more angry. The boat went up and down, and when it came down I thought we were going to go under. It was cold and everyone was wet, and the children were crying. Everyone was frightened, and they were all praying, "God help us. The ocean is angry. God save us." But the boat was climbing higher and higher, and falling down, down, down into the ocean, and the people were shouting, "We are going to die! We are going to die!"

'I saw five people, a man and four women. They were standing together and writing something on a piece of paper. The boat was climbing up and falling down, and I went over to them. I was holding onto people and stumbling, but I wanted to know what they were doing, and when I reached them they told me, "We are writing a letter to the angel of the ocean," and they showed me what they were writing: "Angel of the ocean, please help us. Angel of the ocean, please look after our children. Angel of the ocean, do not be angry. Angel of the ocean, do not leave us. Angel of the ocean, please save us." And they folded up the paper and threw it into the water.

'In the morning it was quiet and the captain came down to tell us we have been at sea for thirty hours, and in six hours we are going to be on Christmas Island. The ocean was resting and everyone was happy. The children started to shout, "Look at the dolphins." The dolphins were jumping around us, and the children were jumping with them, but something in my soul told me we are not going to arrive on Christmas Island.

'After four hours, the engine broke down and the crewmen tried to fix it. One man told me they tried to close a hole with a pair of jeans, with clothing. Suddenly a woman shouted, "The water is coming. We are going to sink, we are going to die!" I couldn't believe it. I looked down and saw the water coming into the boat, coming over our feet, touching our legs, coming quickly.

'I wanted to say goodbye to my son. I wanted to hug him, but the boat went down quickly, as if someone had taken me and pulled me into the ocean. I went down into the water. And when I came up, the gates of hell opened.'

Umm Khultum holds me spellbound. She retains one note and extends it to the very limits. The audience is exalted, their response visceral. In her voice I hear Amal's insistence, and in the song's repetitions, the phrases that Amal would return to in each telling: 'My brother, you can't imagine. When the boat went down I was like a camera. I saw everything. It was ten past three in the afternoon. I know because the watches stopped at that time. My son said, "Forgive me, mother. Maybe I will see you in paradise." The children. They looked fresh. They looked like birds. They looked like they are going to fly in the water. My brother, you can't imagine.'

I cannot fathom how Amal resurfaced, and how for years she had willed herself with each telling to return through the gates of hell, back to those children sleeping on the water. And as I drive, I reflect upon the rest of the story, the events that ensued after the three boats abandoned her, on the night of October 19, until her rescue, and her arrival in Australia. And the final irony: Amal's death from cancer four and a half years after she was hauled from the ocean.

When the sun rose on the morning of October 20 2001,

Amal still clung to the body of the dead woman. 'I was going up and down, up and down, and I was fighting with the water. I was tired. I was hungry. I was thirsty. I thought, maybe my son died. I thought no one is going to save me. All the people had disappeared and there was no one. Just sky and water, birds and dolphins, and I said, "Forgive me, but I want to die."

'I wanted to go quickly. I tried to swallow water, but I couldn't. My brother, believe me, I wanted to go quickly, and I tried to swallow water. I tried to kill myself, but I couldn't. I looked up and saw birds, and it seemed like they were talking to me. I asked myself, "Why are these birds shouting? What do these birds want to tell me?"

'Then I heard the noise of a motor, and I heard voices. I could not believe what I was hearing. I thought, maybe I am dreaming. I turned around, and I saw a boat, and I thought maybe I am going crazy. Then I thought, maybe this is what the birds were shouting. Maybe this is what the birds were telling me. Maybe they showed the Indonesian fishermen my body. Maybe the birds saved me.

'A man came down into the water to help me, and I said, "Please, please, can you take the woman I am holding?" And he said, "No, we did not come to save dead bodies." I let go of the woman and I said to her, "My sister, thank you, you saved my life. You stayed with me all night." I said, "My sister, please forgive me. Maybe I will see you in paradise."

'When they lifted me into the boat I saw many people; but I did not see my son, and I started shouting, "My poor son, I have lost you." Someone told me, "I saw your son in the water. He was holding a piece of wood with other people." I ran to the captain and I begged him, "Please look for my son." He said, "I have too many people." He said, "There are no more people in the water. I must go back to Jakarta."

'I shouted, "You must look for my son." I shouted, "Please. I am a mother, you must help me." I shouted, "Please, you must save my son." I shouted and shouted because I am a mother. I shouted until the captain said, "Okay. Okay! We are going back. We are going to search! For just one hour."

'Soon after, I saw my son on a big wave. I could not believe it. He was holding onto a piece of wood. It looked like he came back to me from the sky. His body had blood all over it because the wood had nails, but the wood saved him. I hugged him, and I said, "Oh my son, welcome back to life again. My son, I love you so much."

'He slept in my arms like a small bird, and I fell asleep and dreamed of a shark swimming next to me, and when I woke up, I saw it was not a shark, but my son lying against me. I looked around the boat, at the people. They were staring at the sky, or at the ocean. Some were asleep, many were weeping. And I asked, "What happened to them? What happened to us?"

'I fell asleep again and in my dream I saw the children. They were pulling my hair, and they were asking me, "What happened to us? What happened to us? Tell the truth. Tell the truth. What happened to us?" And they began flying.

'I woke up from my dream and I saw a girl sitting near me. Her name was Zainab, she was twelve years old, and she was shaking and crying, and I asked her, "Why are you crying?" and she said, "I lost all my family. We were six brothers and sisters, a father and mother. I lost all my family." And I told her, "I am your mother now. I am your family. You are going to stay with me. I will look after you."

'After two days we arrived in Jakarta, and Indonesian immigration officials came and took us to prison, but when we told them our story, they called the United Nations and UN people came and took care of us. Then the Iraqi ambassador came and said, "Salaam, how are you," and he told us that Saddam said we must go back to our country. He said, "There is an aeroplane waiting for you."

'We were very scared. We were praying and crying. A man from the Pakistan embassy was very angry, and he said to the Iraqi ambassador, "Why do you treat people like this? Leave them alone. They have lost their families. They are in shock. They don't want to go back with you."

'We were taken to a hotel, and people came from all over the world to hear our story. One woman told them that dolphins saved her. The dolphins touched her, and pushed her to the boat. She said it was a miracle.

'Zainab stayed with me in the same room. She had an uncle in Sydney. I told her, "You must go to Australia. You must join your uncle. You must study English. You must become something. Your family was fighting for your future. They escaped from Iraq to save you. Don't lose your future."

'When she received a visa for Australia, she said, "Mother, I want to give you a present," and she gave me her watch. The watch had not moved from ten past three. It had not moved since the boat went down in the water, and Zainab said, "Mother, when you look at this watch you will remember me."

'The United Nations said the Australian government was going to give me a visa because my husband was in Melbourne. We waited for seven months, and we became very frightened. We thought they would not take us. In June they told us we can go and we were very happy.

'I cut some flowers and I took them with me. I wanted to bring flowers to my new country. When I arrived with Amjed in Melbourne airport, I saw a man waiting for us. He worked for immigration, and he told me the Australian government had given me a five-year temporary visa. He told me that with this visa I could not leave the country. He told me that maybe after five years I would be sent back to Iraq.

'I could not move. I could not visit my daughter. I could not see my father. I could not bring my older son Ahmed. It was like they put me in jail for five years. I could not believe it.

'The man from immigration told me, "There are some people waiting for you from television and the newspapers. Don't open your mouth. Don't say anything. Don't make any problems." He said, "Come with me and I will take you to your husband. He is waiting."

'When I saw my husband I felt very strange. I had not seen him for a long time. When I saw him I thought he had changed. He looked like a stranger. Maybe something was changed in me. Maybe something changed in the ocean. I told him, "Maybe I am not your wife. Maybe your wife is still in the water. Maybe your wife did not arrive in Australia. Maybe I am a ghost."

'He could not understand what had happened to me. Only the people who were in the water could understand me. I tried to be busy. I started learning English. I started to know the city. I used the train. I used the tram. I used the bus. I started to learn the computer. But when the day was finished I missed my family. I could not see my daughter because if I left Australia I would lose my visa. I could not go back, and I could not go to the future, and at night I could not forget the people in the water.

'Sometimes I think the people who drowned were lucky. Maybe the victims are the ones who are still alive, because they cannot forget what happened. We escaped from Saddam's regime, but sometimes I think his hand is still following us, still touching us.

'After one year in Australia I started to feel sick, and the doctors told me I had breast cancer. I thought I was going to lose my life but they told me they are going to save me. Everything changed in my life. I had chemotherapy. I was losing my hair. I was losing myself.

'There was a big room in the hospital for chemotherapy, where they gave the people drugs. The chemotherapy made my body dry. On the day I had my operation I was very scared. On the ocean I lost my soul, and in Melbourne I was losing my body.'

Umm Khultum is singing, building to a crescendo, and the inner city lights can be seen in the distance. I drive towards them and think of Amal riding the train to the city in the evening, in the company of strangers, staving off sleep and the return of her dreaded dreaming, and the fear she would never again see her absent children.

Amal was one of forty-five survivors of the sinking and, in the months after their rescue, thirty-eight were granted visas: to Norway, Sweden, Finland and Denmark, Canada and New Zealand. Seven survivors were allocated to Australia, allowing them to reunite with relatives who had preceded them.

Those who were assigned elsewhere received permanent visas immediately, in recognition of their trauma and the horror that had afflicted them. The seven survivors assigned to Australia received temporary visas, a predicament that compounded their trauma and cast them back into limbo. Then—three years later—a simple act of acceptance.

Amal was in hospital when she was notified. A nurse handed her the phone. At first she could not understand what the caller was saying. She was disoriented from the illness and its treatment. 'Immigration told me they changed my visa, and I asked them, "What do you mean?" They told me, "We have given you a permanent visa!" I shouted, "A permanent visa, I can't believe it." I cried. I shouted. "Oh God, I am going to see my son, I am going to see my father. I am going to see my daughter. I am going to see my grandchildren. God bless you."

'I was shouting and the nurses were running. They thought something was wrong. I told them what had happened, and they were happy. It was like a miracle. I told them I have my permanent visa and I can see my family. I have my permanent visa and I can fight to bring my son here, I can fight to bring my daughter and her children. My God, I have my visa. I am a free woman in a free country.'

Within months Amal was on a flight to the Middle East. She returned to Melbourne three months later in a wheelchair. The following day she was back in hospital. Days later, as I walked from the car I felt that air of unreality, of time winding down, that I often feel when approaching an ill friend in hospital. I was entering a zone in which time seems suspended, a variant of limbo.

Amal was seated on her bed when I entered. I was surprised by a change in her appearance. She was wearing brightly coloured robes embroidered with images of flowers. Her headscarf was removed and her hair was flowing.

It was the first time I had seen her face uncovered. Her tresses of black hair had strength and lustre despite the ravages of her illness. She seemed unburdened, careless almost. She had something of the youthful spirit and playfulness of the seven-year-old who walked with her father on the banks of the Tigris.

Fearing I had transgressed by seeing her with her hair uncovered, I turned to leave. 'My brother, it doesn't matter,' she said. 'It is not important. People are more important than this. I like the people here. I am sure many people will be at my funeral. I am not afraid. After I die, the birds will keep singing.'

Amal reached for her handbag and took out some photos taken on her recent journey. 'My brother, you can't imagine,' she said, holding the photos, 'when I was coming back to Australia, I read a sign at the airport, "Dubai to Melbourne", and I was very happy. I felt like I was coming home. In the jet I heard a woman talking with an Australian accent. I wanted to hug this woman. I told her I also have a home in your country. I also have a country. I have a family waiting for me.

'When I arrived in Melbourne I was very sick. I went to hospital and the doctor told me that the cancer had spread to my bones and my liver. I told him, "Please, I don't want chemotherapy. What are you going to save? The cancer is all through my body. I don't think you can help me. I don't feel hopeless or sad, but this is the truth. I am going to die and I must be ready."'

She hands me the photos of her daughter Manal, taken at the airport on the day of her arrival in Oman, and photos of her grandchildren. Manal is married to a Palestinian. They first met in Jordan and in recent months had moved to Oman where he had been offered a job as a sports journalist. They have four children.

'I want to tell you a story about my grandson Yanal. He is eight. When I saw him, he looked exactly like my son, Amjed. He hugged me and he ran away. I did not see him for a long time. The next day a journalist came and I told her the story of the boat. I told her everything and they put the story in an Arabic magazine, *El Magili.*'

Amal rummages through the drawer next to the bed, and takes out a printed page and unfolds it. The article is dated November 15 2005. The script is in Arabic, and there is a photo of Amal. 'My daughter's neighbours, six women, came to see me, and they brought me food and clothing, they brought me presents, and they said, "When we read your story we wanted to give you something. We wanted to cry with you. You are a brave woman."

'When we were talking, Yanal came to me. He was very upset, and he was angry. He told me that he had an argument with a boy who did not believe the story about his grandmother. He did not believe I was the woman who survived in the water. The boy said to Yanal, "You are a liar."

'I told Yanal, "Call your friend and bring him inside." He brought him to me. He was a little boy and he was wearing glasses. Yanal said to him, "This is Amal, my grandmother. She saved her life. The boat sank. She was in the water, and she saved her life. I am not a liar."

'I told the boy about the dead woman who saved me. I told him about the children in the water. I told him about the whales and the dolphins. I told him about the shark who swam so close I almost touched him. I told him that I saw my son returning on a wave from the sky back to the ocean. As I talked his eyes were growing wider. He said, "I am sorry. I will tell all my friends about the woman who saved her life in the water."

'After one month, I left my daughter and flew to Iran to see Ahmed. It was too dangerous to meet my family in Baghdad. We planned to meet in Ahmed's flat in Tehran. I waited two weeks for my family. I was scared they would not get out of Iraq, that they would not give them a visa. For eight years I had not seen them. Then my father arrived with three of my brothers. One of them came with his wife and daughter, and my father brought my sister and her nine-year-old son Ali.

'Ali stared at the running water in the bathroom. He could

not believe there was running water. He could not believe there was electricity. He could not believe that when we were sleeping there were no bombs, no terror. He said, "We are in paradise."

'My family's skin colour was strange. Yellow. In Baghdad they did not have enough good food. On the first day they walked like zombies and they did not know they were like this. My father was very sick. He looked very old. He walked very slowly with a stick. I did not want to tell him I was sick. I did not want him to worry.

'I went with them to the beach. I tried to make myself look healthy. My father told me, "I can't believe you fought with the ocean." I told him, "Father, don't worry, the ocean is soft." My sister and brother went to play in the sea, and they looked back at me and said, "We are going to kill the ocean. We are going to ask the ocean, why did you try to kill our sister?" They wanted to make me happy.

'They said, "Baghdad is dangerous. It does not matter which people are in the government, they are all thieves. They want to steal the oil. The only ones who do not have oil are the people. We wait for oil in queues for hours. We open a gas cylinder for cooking and we are afraid we will never have another cylinder. We cut down trees for heating and now there are no more trees in our suburb. We go to the stream for water. It takes us three hours to go there and return. We see dead dogs in the water."

'My brother's little girl is eleven, and she said to me, "Auntie, I want to go with you. I want to go to school. I want to be something. Please take me with you." She was afraid. One of her friends was kidnapped. It was dangerous in Baghdad.

'On the last day we went to the mountains near Tehran. The children played in the snow. On the bus Ali was very sad. He did not want to go back to Baghdad. When he came to Iran he was free. He could talk, he could shout, he could go outside. He was not worried that someone might kill him or kidnap him.'

Amal pauses. She folds up the newspaper and returns it with the photos to her handbag. 'My brother, there is something I must tell you. Something changed in me in Oman, in Tehran. I fought with the ocean. I fought with people smugglers. I fought with immigration to give me a permanent visa. And I was right. Everyone in this hospital is an angel. Australian people have been kind. They help. They help people. I want to tell you something: I started to love Australia.

'Before I went to Oman I told my husband and my son, "When I die, bury me in Iraq." I told them, "I don't want you to bury my body here. If I die please send my body to Baghdad, to my family. I want to sleep near my mother and my two dead brothers. Yesterday I told my husband and my son, "Bury me in Australia."

'I said, "You must forget everything, because there is no Iraq. It is over." I want my children to stay here. I want them to bury me here. They are going to have something here. They are going to put a big stone over me, in this earth, in this safe country.

'When I was in Dubai I heard Australian people talking. I was happy. I wanted to hug them. My brother, when they gave me a five-year protection visa they killed me. And when they gave me a permanent visa, I came back to the living.

I saw Amal for the final time two months later in the last house she rented, the house in which she hoped to receive her older son Ahmed, whose arrival was imminent. She lay in bed, defiant, two days before her passing, refusing to eat, refusing to be shifted to a palliative care unit. She opened her eyes when she heard me entering the bedroom. She was making an effort, willing herself to be lucid.

'My brother, it is good to see you,' she said, lifting her head from the pillow. She talked of her hopes for her son Ahmed who, she had learned just days earlier, had finally obtained a visa, and would soon be flying from Tehran to Melbourne. She was holding on for the day of his arrival, to be at the airport to welcome him.

She hoped to bring her daughter and grandchildren, and other members of her family to Australia. She knew she was dying, but she talked of the future, talked until she lapsed into a sleep that I hoped would be dreamless.

The following day, Amal had consented, after the entreaties of her family and doctor, to be shifted to a hospice. From her room on the last evening she watched the sun set over the city. The dome of the exhibition buildings reminded her of the domes of Baghdad. Amal Basry died on March 18 2006, a warm Saturday afternoon in autumn.

Days later we gathered in the forecourt of the Fawkner Mosque. As we waited for the arrival of the hearse I talked to Faris Khadem, another survivor of the sinking. He said that when the three boats disappeared, he gave up hope. He no longer cared whether he lived or died. He had lost his wife Leyla and his seven-year-old daughter, Zahra. He saw them disappear from his outstretched arms into the ocean.

The thought of seeing his son, who was already in Australia, had kept him afloat. But his desire to survive was crushed when the three boats that had appeared in the night vanished.

He had turned onto his back, placed his hands behind his head, let the life jacket support him, and settled back on the surface of the water as if it were a mattress. He no longer cared if he was dead or living. He closed his eyes and drifted off to sleep, and when he woke, the sun was rising.

He heard the hum of a motor and saw a fishing boat approaching. The crew dragged him from the water. He was the first to be rescued. He saw other survivors clinging to debris, their strength ebbing, and he helped drag them one by one from the ocean.

Late morning they sighted Amal clinging to the bloated corpse. The crew failed in their first attempt to lift her on board the vessel. She was too heavy. They lowered a tyre to retrieve her and Faris went down to help her. They were hauled back on board together.

Faris heard her frantically asking her fellow survivors about her son, Amjed. He saw her pleading with the captain. She would not stop until the captain agreed to search for that extra hour. He witnessed her son's rescue and the reunion between mother and son, an embrace that just one hour earlier had seemed impossible.

In Jakarta, Amal became the mother of the bereaved survivors. She cared for her son. She cared for the girl Zainab. She cared for them all. In the months after the rescue, she visited

Faris every day to see if he was well, and to give him comfort in his grief. She visited everyone. She was concerned for their health, for their despair and their hopelessness. She moved about in her black hijab with that urgent expression I would come to know so well, but her face softened instantly whenever she talked to the children.

It was in those first weeks after the sinking that she began to tell her story. To officials, to journalists, to diplomats, to anyone who would listen. Overnight she became the teller of the story, the one who sought to make sense out of the calamity.

Faris's recollections brought to mind stories of people whose hair had turned white overnight after extreme tragedy. Amal's hair retained its colour, but talking with Faris I came to understand that in clinging for over twenty hours to the corpse in the ocean, Amal had aged many years. Overnight she had become the Ancient Mariner.

The hearse entered the forecourt mid-morning. The coffin was lifted onto the shoulders of the pallbearers and the crowd followed it into the mosque, chanting. They placed the coffin on the carpeted floor and performed the ritual prayers.

Behind the partition wall, hidden from view, women were weeping. A mudlark flew in through the open door and over the mourners. It paused on the chandelier and darted past a banner embroidered with the Quaaba of Mecca.

The coffin was driven to the cemetery, to the Islamic quarter. The children ran about in the sun, the women squatted by the coffin, Korans in hand, chanting, while the men stood around the grave attending to the burial. Amal's body, clothed in a white shroud, was lifted from the coffin and lowered into the ground to Amjed, who had climbed down to receive it. His task was to arrange the body in accordance with tradition: right side resting on the earth, head facing Mecca. The men lowered a mixture of earth and water to Amjed to fix the body in the correct position.

Amal was buried to the chatter of birds, the laughter of children, and the murmur of prayers and conversation. This was how she would have wished it.

Ten days later, Amal's older son, Ahmed, arrived in Melbourne. The brothers had rarely been apart until they were separated in Iran, Amjed told me as we waited for Ahmed to clear customs. They had not spent any time away from Amal until she was forced to choose who would go with her on that ill-fated journey.

In the five years since, Amjed had been burdened by guilt at being the one chosen. There were times he wished he had not survived the sinking. When Ahmed stepped through the arrivals gate, the brothers embraced and wept.

Now, almost five years since Ahmed's arrival, I am driving into the centre of the city. I am nearing the completion of my promise. I cast my thoughts back to a phone call that I received one night from Amal.

'My brother, I cannot sleep. I must tell you something. When I was a girl I asked my father, "Can I be a singer?" And he told me, "This is not a good idea. It is a hard life. It is not a good life for a woman." He loved Umm Khultum. He loved music.

He sang to me when we walked by the Tigris, but he told me it was not good for me to be a singer. Sometimes I think if I had become a singer my life would have been better.'

I now see that, in ways she would never have wished for or imagined, Amal was the voice of those who survived and those who perished in the ocean. Her voice resonated with the power of Umm Khultum's. Like her idol, she possessed a charisma that drew people to her. She was a consummate performer, recounting her tales with an incessant beat, a mesmerising rhythm. From quiet but intense beginnings, she built towards a state of *tarab*, of union between teller and listener.

I park the car in the inner city and set out, as Amal had done, from Flinders Street Station. The footpaths on Princes Bridge are crowded with peak-hour commuters. I descend the stone steps to the river. On this warm evening the riverside bar is overflowing with after-work drinkers, but I am focused on the banks opposite, at the palm trees rising from the lawns that slope down to the water.

I walk from the bridge on the concrete walkway, and step onto the sandy path beneath the Moreton Bay figs that line this side of the riverbank. I am beyond the busyness, but still in touch with the city.

I sit on the bench beneath the figs, where Amal sat, and look at the palms across the water, diagonally opposite. The sight of the palms from this bench, Amal once told me, was the goal of her night wanderings. It returned her to Baghdad, to the banks of the Tigris.

I think of her on the morning she came upon the gathering

of weeping people and learned that a person can float long after they have ceased living. I see the fire in her eyes. She is haunted by what she had endured on the ocean.

And I hear her voice: 'My brother, I cannot sleep. I just woke up from a dream. In the dream I am walking towards a door. It is the door to paradise. I open the door, and inside it is light. Everything is white, and I see the people who drowned, the three hundred and fifty-three men, women and children. They are together, they are laughing. They are happy and they are calling to me. "Come join us. Come join us."

'I want to go with them. I start to walk towards them, but I stop. I cannot leave the story of the children who are lying on the ocean, and of the women and their sons and daughters. I cannot forget what the ocean did to them. I must wake up. I must tell everyone what happened. My brother, this is what my life is for. To tell what happened.'

AUTHOR'S NOTE

The stories in this collection range in time from 1970 to 2011. In several stories I have combined separate incidents and encounters into one composite tale and/or one composite character. These include: 'The Music Box', 'Bella Ciao', 'Capriccio', 'The Wall' and 'A Chorus of Feet'. The names of characters depicted in these stories and some details have been changed to protect the anonymity of people I have lost touch with. The real names remain, with permission, in 'Violin Lessons', 'The Partisan's Song' and 'The Ancient Mariner'. 'The Ancient Mariner' is based on my many conversations with Amal Basry, and on additional material from filmmaker Steve Thomas's interviews with Amal. One of Amal's brothers, Dr Sahir Hassan Basry, has a different account of the death of their brother Bahir, which appears on the website sievx.com

I made use of the following books: Frederick Taylor, *The Berlin Wall*, Bloomsbury, London, 2006; John Berger and Jean Mohr, *A Seventh Man*, Penguin Books, Baltimore, 1975; Timothy Snyder, *Bloodlands: Europe between Hitler and Stalin*, Bodley Head, London, 2010; Thomas Mann, *Death in Venice*, translated by Kenneth Burke, Stinehour Press, New York, 1972; Michael Herr, *Dispatches*, Picador, London, 1978; Nadine Cohodas, *Princess Noire: the tumultuous reign of Nina Simone*, Panther Books, New York, 2010.

For additional information I am indebted to: Michael Rubbo, *Sad Song of Yellow Skin*, documentary film, 1970; Steve

Thomas, *Hope,* Flying Carpet Films, 2007; *Something to Declare,* Actors for Refugees; Marg Hutton's website sievx.com

Song credits include: 'Pirate Jenny', lyrics by Bertolt Brecht for *The Threepenny Opera,* 1928, adapted into English by Marc Blitzstein, 1954; Hirsh Glik, 'Never Say', 1943, and 'Quiet the Night', 1943; Shmerl Kaczerginsky, 'Quiet, Quiet', 1943; Mordechai Gebirtig, 'Our Town Is Burning', 1936; Y. Shpigel, 'Close Your Little Eyes', circa 1943; 'Bella Ciao' was a popular song of the Italian resistance, and is based on a much older folk song sung by the rice growers of the Po Valley.

I received valuable feedback from Richard Freadman, Majid Shokor, Naji and Myra Cohen, Mimi Kluger, Sonia Torly, Rose Offman, Gabrielle Fakhri, Alice Garner and Phillip Maisel. I thank Marg Hutton, Faris Khadem, Julian Burnside, Kate Durham, Dennis Sikiotis, Ephthimios and Aleka Varvarigos, Kavisha Mazzella, Abbas Al Shiakhly, Anne Horrigan-Dixon, Kon Karapanagiotidis, the Basry family, Graham Reilly and Helen Kokkinidis.

I thank Michael Heyward of Text for his perceptive advice and support, Jane Pearson, who edited the book with great skill and insight, and Chong Weng Ho for the striking cover design. The Literature Board of the Australia Council provided material support.

I thank my wife Dora and my son Alexander, who have supported me in many ways, as always.

'Evocative, charismatic and moving.'
Australian

'An affectionate recreation of the inner-
Melbourne suburb of Carlton in 1958...
Ultimately optimistic and affirming.'
Sydney Morning Herald

'Such a rewarding read...Readers are left
with a great deal to think about.'
Canberra Times

textpublishing.com.au

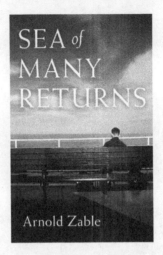

SEA of MANY RETURNS

Arnold Zable

'When I had finished *Sea of Many Returns*,
I turned back to the beginning and started again.
It's a fabulous book.'
Canberra Times

'Superbly crafted, at times exhilarating and edifying.'
Australian

'Zable has a remarkable gift…He holds pain with
unsettling gentleness. His prose is such good company
that you accept its honesty.'
Age

textpublishing.com.au